Who
On Earth Is
Happening?

The thoughts we choose
to think are the tools
we use to paint the canvas
of our lives.

Happy Holiday, and all the

Best for 1994.

Barbara. x

What On Earth Is Happening?

A SPIRITUAL VISION OF A WORLD IN CRISIS

Nick Bamforth
Denise Cooney & Dr. Eric Morse

AMETHYST BOOKS
NEW YORK   LONDON

Published in the United States by Amethyst
Books, P.O. Box 895, Woodstock,
N.Y. 12498
and in the United Kingdom by Amethyst
Books, Lime Treet House, Swalcliffe,
Banbury, Oxon OX15 5EH.

ISBN 0–944256–05–8

Amethyst Books are distributed in the United
States by The Talmon Co., New York
and in the United Kingdom by Ashgrove
Distribution, Bath.

Contents

Foreword

For so many people, the events in the world at large and in our own personal lives appear to be totally random, even out of control. With the changes in climate, the situation in the Middle East and a gradual realization that the material world of economic boom is becoming an illusion of the past, fear is increasingly beginning to dominate our lives: a fear of losing what stability we have, but, most strongly of all, a fear of the unknown.

There are others, however, who know deep down that the changes that are happening both in the outside world and within themselves are part of something greater which cannot be fully understood by our rational minds, but which we feel to be as real as the physical world we experience with our own senses. It is a consciousness, an awareness that something is happening on this planet of ours which goes far beyond anything we have ever experienced within our living memory, indeed within the living memory of mankind. It is the knowledge, also, that there has been set in motion a process of change which will leave no life unaffected and will fundamentally change the world we live in, our attitude to our fellow men and our perception of the brief span of time which we call our life in this physical form.

The purpose of this book is to bring these changes into perspective, so that those of you who wish to see a better and more just world can begin to see the light at the end of what seems to be an endlessly dark tunnel. It is also to give an understanding that all the turmoil you have been going through in your own life and which you see around you in the lives of others is part of a process of growth, however painful it may be, towards the realization of your highest potential, the core of your being which you know to be your true self.

This is no longer a time to live your life through the eyes of others, conforming to the conditioning of the society around you. It is a time to use your own judgment about your own life and to follow your own intuition rather than follow the flock like a sheep.

We do not say that this final decade of the millennium will be easy, for it will not be, just as any fundamental change is not easy. However, you will find that old ways of behavior and of viewing life will begin to fail you in this changing world; it is then that your intuition, your own inner knowledge can be your only guide.

All three of us who have written this book have tried, as best as we can, to live our lives according to our own conscience and this has often met with some resistance from those who tell us that we ought to behave in this way or that way. Following your own spiritual path can be lonely and hard, but there comes a point when you know that there is no other way.

In this book, each of us, in our own way, will give you an impression of what really is happening on this planet and within our own lives. Each of us shares the same fundamental beliefs, but the style and content of our writing is as different as our personality and background. We hope that you will feel in tune with some part of this book and that you will feel free to write to one or all of us through the publisher.

1

What On Earth Is Happening?

The Inner Self

Nick Bamforth

It is a sad world we live in, where pride and greed rule those who govern us and where we, the masses, sit back and grumble about them without understanding that it is the responsibility of each individual to create the world around them. In this, democracy is barely different from dictatorship. We exercize our right to vote every few years and then sit back and allow a small hierarchy of power to make the major decisions which affect the world and our own lives. Those who govern a country are a mere reflection of the masses whom they govern – people who are indifferent to the fate of mankind or the planet as a whole; people who have become so deeply embedded in the material world that they have lost sight of any reality beyond it.

The crisis which exists today is not merely a crisis of war or of economic decline; it is The Crisis, the turning point of humanity. Whether we choose to continue along the path of egotism, materialism and callous disregard for our fellow living beings is a matter of choice. And this is not a choice that can be made for us by those who govern us; it is a choice which we all must make within ourselves.

The war in the Gulf was a symbol of the powers which we have by our indifference permitted to gain control in our world. On one side, there is a meglomaniac, a man who is obsessed with his personal power to the exclusion of all else, a man who is prepared to destroy with the vilest weapons even a segment of his own population. On the other hand, there is a global power which is the essence of materialism. Its culture is built on the ethic of accumulating personal, material wealth, blind to its effect on those both within and beyond its own population who do not share in this wealth and blind to the havoc it wreaks on the environment of the planet which supports us. And the focal point of this war is oil, a natural product of our Earth which is extracted without anything put back in return and which is then transmuted into substances and gases which are throwing this same Earth into imbalance.

We have strayed so far from any innate connection with the Earth and the Universal Energy of which we are all part that we have been unable to listen to, see or feel the extent to which we have led to the brink of destruction not only the human race, but all other living creatures who share this planet with us. The Earth as an organism is immensely powerful and resilient; it does not need humanity as we need it. Whether we as a race survive is, in the long term, a matter of supreme indifference to the Earth as a whole. Just as there were many forms of life before us, there can be many after us.

However, at this time, our fate is inextricably linked with that of the Earth as a whole, for we have, whether we like it or not, reached that stage in our evolution where we have dominion over our fellow creatures and where we have the choice to use this responsibility wisely or otherwise. There are those who believe that we are doomed to fail and to destroy ourselves; there are others who say that such fears of destruction are exaggerated and that there is nothing wrong with the way that we live.

It all comes down to the way we view progress. Most people see progress in purely material terms, creating a better material life for ourselves or maybe the world as a whole; they look with pride at human achievement as one invention spawns another and each generation is able to have a more comfortable life than the previous one. Our Western society pays homage to this ethic, as we flock to make more money, to become more secure and maybe do a little better than our next door neighbour.

Then there are other more concerned people who see the inequality and injustice of the world around them, and try, within this system, to contribute more to the welfare of others. They are the ones who understand the enormity of what we are doing to our environment and to the world as a whole and, through the new Green consciousness, try to create changes on the physical plane.

Yet, what even the Green consciousness does not fully take into account is the dimension which exists beyond our physical world: that 'spiritual' part of us which is connected to God, the Universe, the Source of All Being or whatever you wish to call it. This has little to do with religion in the traditional sense; it is the understanding that we are an integral part of a Whole which lies far beyond our understanding.

Spiritual consciousness is not something which can be taught, as it is only something that an individual can feel for himself or herself. Just as anything you read in this book will either feel right to you or seem a load of rubbish, your connection to this greater Whole is inherently felt within you or it is not. Whatever is written in this book cannot be subjected purely to the rational mind; it is also appealing to your intuitive nature which knows when something is right for you – not necessarily for everyone, but for you personally.

However, once you have that sense within yourself of a reality beyond the physical world which we experience in our earthly existence, there is no turning back, as this new vision opens up a completely new way of looking at one's own life and its place in the greater scheme of things. I am not talking about the view of God as propagated by orthodox religion in which He is some omnipotent being separate from us or even in our midst; I am talking about the God Within us, that eternal connection within all of us to the greater Whole which is the Source of our being. The idea of a separate God breeds the belief in an external fate over which we as individuals have no control; a sense of connection to the greater Whole ultimately brings us to the understanding that we are able to create our own individual reality, and, in doing so, affect the world around us.

To make this shift in consciousness is by no means easy, as it makes us take responsibility for our every action; as soon as we begin to feel this deeper connection to the Whole, we cannot avoid assuming this responsibility, for there would otherwise be no point in existing on this earthly plane. When one begins to see the infinite connections of life and to understand the eternal nature of one's own being, there is no alternative but to live one's life to the fullest and to act according to one's own principles and feelings rather than accept the norms which society tries to impose upon us. As we shall see in the second section of this book, the so-called values of our Western society which have brought us to the present point of crisis are based on old precepts which have nothing to do with the diverse and ever changing world we live in today.

For many people, as was the case with myself, it can be an encounter with death which reopens the spiritual channels within us. The one thing of any certainty in our human lives is that we shall all at some point die, yet it is amazing how little this fact is confronted until it is forced upon us, whether through our own mortality or the death of someone near to us. For those who do not believe in a reality beyond this earthly plane, death has a finality to it which ultimately invokes fear. Even within the Christian religion, the harsh idea of the judgment of an external God together with the hazy notion of Heaven and Hell is hardly something to look forward to! However, if you feel that death of our physical body is an essential transformation from one reality to another, like passing through a veil, this transition holds no fears, as it is a continuation of the eternal cycle of which we are all part.

Once more, the fact that I write this out of my own inner conviction only means that this is true for me. It is only true for you if you feel it within yourself. Much of the certainty I feel comes from the work I have done with terminally ill patients, and many of the experiences I have shared with them as they approach death, in particular the wonderful sense of release which I have seen come over them, have been among the most powerful of my life.

Living in the physical body can be both rewarding and painful, but, in either case, we cannot help but change and grow as we go through our lives, especially if we act with consciousness. One could almost say that we are trapped within our physical bodies, for we cannot just run away from all the events and relationships which confront us throughout our lives. Every aspect of our being must be dealt with and worked through – if we choose to, we can certainly turn our backs and bury our heads in the sand, but whatever comes to challenge us in our lives will ultimately not disappear until we face it and, if necessary, integrate it into our being.

Every spiritual master, from Christ and Buddha to the many we have never heard of, has acknowledged the existence of the dark side – that part of us which has become separated from our spiritual, all-encompassing nature. Throughout our evolution, the consciousness of humanity has expanded as we have forged ahead using our innate creativity and free will to shape the world we live in, and part of the cost of this process has been to lose the sense of unity between all things. As our world has become one of judgmental duality, of good and evil or intellect and intuition, we have learnt to judge parts of ourselves, thereby splitting them away from us and giving them an energy of their own, rather than integrating them into the whole of our being.

The state in which we find ourselves today is a culmination of this process on the external plane. Instead of seeing the unity and connection between all living creatures, we focus on our differences, treating them with a lack of understanding which arises from fear. The conflicts which exist throughout the world are filled with judgment and self-righteousness, where one side sees itself as right and the other wrong, with all shades of grey in between of no relevance. Instead of seeking common ground, our increasingly egoistic, and also fearful, leaders rush headlong into violence irrespective of its costs to humanity and to the Earth.

What we must of course not do is judge them, as they are, on a magnified scale, merely acting out what most of humanity does in their day-to-day lives, judging our neighbours and acting out our own fears and insecurities, sometimes with a bombast which conceals the feeling of emptiness and separation which lies deep within our race. We must attend to ourselves, and, by doing so, we can create a ripple of change which can, in time, become a tidal wave.

Judgment Day and the Return of the Christ Consciousness

Nick Bamforth

Anyone seeing this heading would be justified in thinking that they were just about to embark on some orthodox Christian tract, but this could not be further from the truth. Christianity in its present form has little to do with the teachings of Christ, and the doomsayers' interpretation of Judgment Day as the end of the world is simplistic and erroneous.

Jesus Christ, like Buddha five hundred years before him, was the bearer of a Consciousness which far transcended him as a man. As men, Buddha and Jesus had a great deal in common. They were both miraculously born from a royal line; they both underwent and overcame temptations of the material life, leading to a renunciation of the old ways and to a new life as a wandering teacher performing miracles (i.e. showing their power over the material world), preaching salvation from within, followed by a small band of disciples.

They both advocated reform within the old religions of Hinduism and Judaism respectively, stressing the personal, spiritual quest rather than the formal adherence to law, charity rather than ascetic prohibitions. They refused to be bound by political structures and social distinctions, renouncing violence and emphasizing the brotherhood of man.

The Christ Consciousness and the Buddha Consciousness are therefore inextricably linked upon this Earth, with one fundamental difference between them which separates the East from the West. While the Buddha sees the material world as 'maya', the world of illusion, and represents enlightenment through disengagement from the physical world through meditation, yoga etc., the Christ Principle is based on the quest of each individual to find his or her own Truth through personal experience in this material world and by means of active interreaction with his or her fellow men through Love.

The essence of Christ the man is that he took spirituality out of the temple and onto the streets so that the masses could find their own spiritual connection to the Source of our Being, the Universe, God or whatever you wish to call the Whole of which we are all part. His essential teachings were that God is Within all of us and God is Love – not just the love we associate with close, personal relationships, but a broader notion of Love, which we express by seeing other people as they are without judgment.

Tied in with love are the equal truths of humility and surrender, of Christ washing his disciples' feet and turning his other cheek. Humility is the understanding that all men are equal, that no one person is superior to another, irrespective of their social or intellectual stature. Surrender is the action of faith, trusting our intuitive connection to the Source – something which is beyond the scope of our rational mind to explain.

I do not need to tell you how far we have strayed from these simple teachings in our modern world. Instead of living our lives according to the Principle of Love, we continuously judge not only others but also ourselves. We live by a code of written and unwritten rules which tells us that we ought to do this or should not behave in that way, to the extent that we have surrendered the individual responsibility of living according to our own conscience or inner Truth. We have created a world of inequality devoid of compassion in which the individual drive to continuously better our material condition has suffocated our deeper spiritual yearnings and our concern for our fellow living beings

— and in this obsessive drive to achieve, the idea of surrender is overwhelmed by the need to control every aspect of our lives.

Traditional religion, the supposed shepherd of our spiritual needs, has lost all connection with Spiritual Consciousness. From India/Pakistan to the Middle East to Northern Ireland, violence is repeatedly committed in the name of religion. The so-called Great Religions have long since developed into monoliths of power, more intent on keeping control of this power by means of immutable 'moral laws' which have no place in an ever changing world, rather than encouraging their flocks to find their own God Within. By promoting the idea of a separate omnipotent God, judging us from above, and by focusing on the sin and unworthiness of man, they are not only contradicting the teachings of Christ and Buddha, but they are using the innate fear and guilt within mankind to separate man from man.

Lying at the heart of this mentality is the triumph of materialism and the rational mind, with the spiritual and intuitive natures of man banished to the subconscious. It is our rational mind which always sees separateness and distinctions between things and people, while our intuitive nature feels the connectedness not only between ourselves and our fellow beings, whether human or otherwise, but also with the Whole which cannot be perceived by our five senses. The rational mind only accepts as valid what is perceived or understood, so that we continue to march on under the illusion that the material world is the only reality; we submerge ourselves more and more within the cocoon of material possessions and are constantly in fear of losing what we have.

The result of this material/rational world is what we see around us: a world of inequality where the few control the many, where there are millions of starving people in a world of abundance; a Western world of material wealth concealing a lack of inner fulfillment and wholeness; an atmosphere of fear, distrust and conflict between groups who perceive only their differences, not their connection; and, finally, an abuse of power and responsibility where we have brought ourselves to the edge of destruction, not only of ourselves, but of the other living creatures over which we have dominion.

This is what Judgment Day is all about: not the judgment by some external, angry god, but the judgment of whether we as individuals wish to cling to the old ways of power and control or guide our world into a new era of love and compassion. However much we may grumble about the powers which govern us, the ultimate responsibility is with humanity as a whole, the teeming mass of individuals each of whom has the power to find their own inner God and live their lives according to their own conscience and intuition. We are indeed on the brink, but we are beings of consciousness and free will, who have the ability to forge our own path.

   This may seem unrealistic to many, but the energy of change at this time is there for all to see and feel. On the one level, there are the momentous changes that have recently occurred and are continuing to occur in the political and social arena – whether they appear 'good' or 'bad' is irrelevant, as they are the result of the momentum of a Greater change which has taken hold on our planet at this time, not only on the external, political plane, but also deep within the psyche of our race as a whole. Most of you who read this book will have been affected by this energy, reflected in the major upheavals which you have recently gone through in your own lives, many of which have been painful, but which have also led you towards a deeper examination of your beliefs and of what is really important to you.

   It is a sad fact of our present condition that we must go through suffering on some level in order to reconnect with that inner part of us which sees beyond the physical world of our senses into a reality which we know is greater than what our rational mind can explain. It is through our emotions that we experience the richness of our human condition and sometimes the intensity of these emotions leads us into a realm which takes us away from the material world and deep into ourselves. This intensity has been becoming stronger and stronger, and sometimes more difficult to bear, for the many people who have had the courage to confront the transformation which has been occurring within them.

This is all part of the shift in energy and the change of vibration which is happening within our planet as a whole. Just as we are an integral part of the Earth, the Earth itself is a living organism which is an integral part of the Solar System and the Universe as a Whole. The Universe, or God, is no static thing which never changes. It is constantly expanding, just as our human consciousness is constantly expanding. The one is tied to the other.

Any scientist will tell you that the basis of our world is vibration and that different substances, or non-substances for that matter, are essentially made up of different vibrations. Each human being emits a different vibration which accounts for certain individuals being attracted or repelled by certain others. In essence, vibration is linked with consciousness: someone who is embedded in the material world without concern for anything beyond his material comfort will have a lower vibration than someone whose life is devoted to the help of others. I must stress though, that, in Universal terms, there is no such judgment as one being 'better' than the other. It is simply a matter of vibration.

There are continuous cycles of change within the Universe and, as any part of It moves from one cycle to another, the frequency of this part's vibration increases at a faster rate. This is exactly what is occurring upon our planet Earth at this very moment and it will ultimately leave not one individual living being unaffected. Those of a more sensitive nature are affected first, as their nervous systems are more attuned to this change in vibration, but also those old tyrannies of control which have governed our world for so long are slowly beginning to feel their power slip away as they suddenly find that they are unable to remain immutable in the face of this greater Universal force. This is why there is change and upheaval already occurring on an individual and international level.

The Earth itself is of course also changing. For centuries, now, man has been interfering with the delicate balance which exists on our planet. The Earth is a formidable organism and has been able to absorb the plundering and the abuse which man has wrought upon it, but it is beginning to reach its limit and, as it raises its own vibration to take up its new position as the Heart Center of our solar system, it can no longer carry around the excess toxins which have been pumped into its body and atmosphere and will begin to recreate its own balance.

The bizarre and extreme weather patterns all over the world are a prelude to even greater Earth changes, which have of course been prophesied in all ancient spiritual traditions. Just as the human body goes into a fever when fighting off an invading organism, so the Earth is beginning to rid itself of those substances and energies which have a damaging effect on its own health and balance. In order for the Earth and humanity as a whole to be able to pass into this new cycle of their growth, a renewed sense of balance and harmony must be restored, or else we will not be able to withstand the change of vibration which is coming upon us. It is as simple as that.

The final decade of this millenium will without doubt be one of great hardship and of the ultimate test. Like a cornered rat, the old way of power and control and materialism knows that its very existence is threatened and will therefore fight to the death to maintain its supremacy, blind to the results of its actions. There will be much suffering, but this does not mean the end of the world; it is the preparation for the new order to come out of the ruins of the old.

If you feel that this is unrealistic and that such things have been said before without coming to fruition, examine your own conscience and see what kind of world you wish to see. The second coming of the Messiah or the Christ has nothing to do with the arrival of a new Saviour; it is the return of the Christ Consciousness – not within just one man, but within the hearts and minds of those who know the Truth of Love and their God Within. Jesus rooted the Christ Consciousness on the Earth; throughout the continuous turmoil and change of the past two thousand years of the Piscean Age, this consciousness has spread – not to all of humanity, but to enough people who know that the time will come to unite their individual energies into a Force of change.

The Earth Changes

Denise Cooney

We have been hearing about the changes that have been predicted by all the great teachers since the beginning of time. What are the Earth Changes? How do they affect us? How can we work with them? And what can we expect of people around us during this time? To understand what is truly meant by the changes, we have to try and open up our minds to the Ancient Teachers and relearn the messages that they have left for us.

Christ spoke extensively of the end of an Age. For some people, it meant the end of the world. For centuries, the church has used this as a tool for the enslavement of people. The thought of going to hell forever and being punished was a great way to control people and to hold back the real information that is meant for everyone.

Still today, people are waiting for that better place to come in the afterlife, so to speak. They use it as an excuse to do whatever comes to mind and then some just glibly say: 'Well, I'll pay for it someday, but not now!'

The Truth is that Christ said there would be signs in the heavens and they would signify the end of an Age. The Book of Revelations is filled with metaphysical meanings that are not as incomprehensible as some would like you to think. However, this is not going to be lessons on how to read the Bible. This is meant as a guide, a complement to the great works that are out and available to all since the beginning of time.

So, how do we define the Earth Changes? If you have never heard of them before or if you are unfamiliar with the terminology, it means different things to different people. No one person is the authority on the Changes. I have read many books on the Changes and have tranced information from my Teachers Michael the Archangel and Sananda on what is to pass. The information all dovetails together at most points but the truth is that no one knows exactly what is going to happen. We can conjecture through astrology or contact my guides or someone else's. We can read about the Hopi Prophecies or the Book of Revelations or Nostradamus. We can run to this teacher or that teacher to find out if Edgar Casey, Sun Bear or Sananda has the real low down on what is to pass during our lifetime or we can take charge of our lives and implement the teachings of truthful, everyday living.

The Earth Changes, as to the best of my ability to convey them to you, are about the physical, emotional, financial, psychological and spiritual changes each and every living thing on the Earth will experience for the next thirty years. According to many sources the changes are the awakening of the hidden source of power that lies within each of us and the release of that power creates a quantum leap for humankind and all the creatures that live on the Earth as well. To the best of my understanding, if we do not pull together as a race, the collective 'group Karma' will create ripples and waves through the different planes of consciousness and, when the effects of this comes into the Earth Plane, there may be tremendous upheaval.

The hidden power I am referring to is the God/Goddess given power that has been with us since the beginning of time. It is the power of the spoken word, the power of the mind. It is creating our reality to be in sync with what we believe we deserve to have. For some, this power, when it is unleashed, will have untold misery. Why? Because we actually have always had control over our own lives but have been too stubborn not to notice this, while we were busy pointing out the flaws in our family, neighbor, husband, wife or lover.

We have been wondering who will get us out of our environmental mess and how we can beat all the politicians at their same game. We have, here in America, land of the free and the brave, been openly pouring out hatred and bigotry to the world, telling people that our freedom and our way of life is the best. Yet, we have not yet reckoned with the Native culture, nature or the countless injustices we all are responsible for whether we are Black, White, Red or Yellow.

That is the power which we all have abused throughout the ages and which is causing the Earth Changes.

The Earth is a living entity. She provides us with air, food, and water. In return, we were to have blessed the Earth for selflessly giving up her resources so that we, as children of the Earth, could be taken care of. At one time we used to use the power of the spoken word to bless all things. To civilized and educated people, the 'backward tribes' that still do this border line on superstition. These educated people can prove scientifically that praying to gods or goddesses is foolish and the sign of an undeveloped mind.

Well, when we prayed to the Earth and to the Spirits which controlled the air, water, land, rain, sun, moon, deer and so on, we had a more balanced life. We learned to watch for signs as the Earth went routinely through times of flooding, earthquakes and other disasters, knowing the power of Mother Nature and respecting that power.

Now, I am not saying that technological advances or medicine are an enemy. The human element has proven time and time again that, when given usage of highly available skills and knowledge, there will be abuse and greed. I would sincerely like to think that this is not the case with all people, but the way the world is today was not caused by just the 'devil' as some would like us to think.

As a race we cannot afford to be short sighted but, for some reason, we are. Maybe, it is the inherent animal behavior that we carry over from successive lifetimes of development which means that we pass through the animal kingdom before we attain human consciousness. Possibly, it is the transfer of those strong 'impressions' that keeps the human race from evolving into a higher state of beingness which is our spiritual birthright.

Somehow, I think that, when we balance the technological and the spiritual element of ourselves, we are truly using the gifts that Spirit has been waiting for us to discover. It is with the correct use of force that we create the Divine. You do not have to wait for this to happen around you. You can create balance by believing in yourself and working on yourself: mind, soul, and body. This is the only way you will get through the coming changes.

Now back to the subject at hand. What are the Changes? The Earth, since the beginning, has been shifting and changing all along. With the onslaught of human technological advances, we have as a whole somehow moved away from the concept of keeping in balance with all living things.

We have been given an assignment if you will. We have been told to grow spiritually and work with the Earth. We have been told that we have free will and that we will be given dominion over all things.

Let's look at it this way. Imagine that you told someone that you trust them enough, without even checking into their background, that they could live in your house, have the keys to your car and hold your bank book which contained your life savings. You also explained that everything you owned was priceless and irreplaceable, so be careful not to destroy anything. You also left your children with them and asked them to take good care of things because you didn't know when you would return. I know this is an impossible scenario – what fool would leave their most precious commodities with a total stranger? Just because you are both human, is that enough to have in common?

Well! That is the modern version of Creation and the Earth Changes that we are in the middle of! When we arrived on the scene here on Planet Earth, we were given a place that was filled with beauty. It provided us with food and endless resources. We were given certain rules to follow. There were those who studied the ways of spirit and they were respected for their wisdom and healing ways. We had

Elders who guided us through many strange and mysterious ways. We also had a matriarchial society. Things were in balance around the World. We were told that we had to be the Guardians of the Earth. In return, the animals would give up their lives for us so that we may eat. We were told to bless their spirit. We did all of this in accordance to the Law.

Then, one day, so to speak, things started to change. People forgot to pray due to the fact that the food was there whether you respected what was provided for you or not. You didn't have to go the ways of the Medicine People because their cures were known and you could take them into your own hands. Why! You could even make money at it. You no longer needed to listen to the ways of the Elders. They were old and who wanted to listen to an old woman or man anyway? They were the signs of weakness. Yes! Things started to change.

Masters still came to Earth to warn the children of God that if you go too far away from home, the very Earth that protects you could turn against you.

Rubbish! How could this massive planet of Earth ever be depleted of clean water, fresh air, forests, fish, animals or plants?! The thought that the atmosphere could allow harmful rays to create disease! Hogwash!

So Christ then returned to the Earth and how did we handle his message that 'I will come as a thief in the night.'? 'Love they neighbor as thyself'; miracles, messages and information about the Earth Changes; how was it received?

With unfortunately typical, animal, human behavior. 'You mean that I must give of myself and not be greedy? Forget this guy; let's get this nut out of here; he's ruining my position . . . there is money to be made . . . what do you mean that I don't have the corner market on God? . . . Kill Him!'

So, this is where we are! We have taken as much as we can from the Earth. We have walked away from being able to be in balance with not only the physical plane but the spiritual planes that are all around us. What can we expect to see?

Think back to that story that I just wrote. Can you imagine coming home and finding your house in a mess, your car a wreck and your poor children in a terrible state? Well, this is what we have done. We have ruined the Earth. We have taken advantage of what was left for us, destroyed species and, even as I write, are destroying the forests of the world at a rapid rate. What would you do to these people that you trusted? Well, this is why things are happening.

For all of our advancement somehow we cannot get it into our thick heads that we are responsible for every action in our lives. Why is science so willing to accept Newton's Law of 'For every action there is an equal and opposite reaction' to be true, without seeing how it pertains to every day existence? For every tree we cut down, a little more erosion occurs. For every bit of chemical we dump into the ocean, a little more pollution occurs in the Seas and therefore affects the life in the Liquid Sky.

The Changes we will see according to my Guidance are the following. This is information that has been given to me over the years and some has come to pass and some has yet to come to pass. Some see that tremendous shifts and changes will occur; others only see that the human spirit will evolve and we will become Light Bodies. What I write here is not set in stone – none of it need happen if human consciousness is suddenly uplifted. It is all down to us, to our free will to change and to grow. This is in accordance to the Laws of Melchezadek and the words of Sananda and Michael. This is paraphrased for some of the language they use is not always easy for all to understand.

We will start seeing that the seasons will change first. Roses will bloom in the winter and crops will not grow when they are supposed to. There will be food shortages due to the changes of the growing seasons. The trees act, in a sense, as the brain of the seasons and with the continuous cutting down of the trees, the energies that are given off from the trees to help influence the weather will be lost. The seasons will have a form of Alzheimer disease – to put it in terms which we might understand. There will be weather all right but none like the sort that we have ever recalled experiencing since the beginning of time. The winds will become very powerful; they will uproot trees and shift and shake down buildings. There will be electrical storms of such proportions that it will affect the very magnetic fields that go around the Earth.

The animals will at the same time be providing miracles and trying to warn people by giving up their lives and doing things to protect people.

The children are to be protected; they will be open to the influences of the spirits around the Earth and the dark side of human nature will enter them. Children will be heavily influenced by the dark side and we must learn to protect them. The dark side is believed to be the darker nature of all things. You cannot run away from the dark side or wish it away. Nor can you say: just don't give it energy for it is always there. It is that side of ourselves that has created this situation in the first place.

The dark side will have power over many people. The teachers of what they call Truth will be leading people into false rays of hope and teaching them convoluted messages. They, however, will be revealed as teachers who have no power.

The Truth will be revealed on every level. All people will be able to see themselves for who they truly are. You will not be able to hide who you are from yourself or anyone. You will be able to see lies as clearly as you see the nose on your face. This will be a very interesting time indeed.

This is why the genuine Teachers have always said 'judge not lest ye be judged'. The very thing you criticize about someone or something else will be your very own undoing, for all will see your critical nature as well as your healing nature. So, if you think people won't be able to see that secret bigot that hides within . . . look out! That goes for everyone, so clean it up now and accept who you are.

The water supply will become contaminated. The fish will become inedible.

There will be massive Earthquakes in Los Angeles and 24 hours after the devastating nature of this, New York City will also be destroyed by an earthquake the size of which will go off the Richter scale. The entire Eastern seaboard of America from Boston to Virginia will be uninhabitable. You must go at least 75 miles inland to find some stable land.

Florida will not be very safe due to the coastal flooding. Arkansas will be fine. However, in Tennesee and other states that have nuclear power plants, there will be explosions due to the fact that most of the power plants are on fault lines. Check this out in your local area.

There will be a stopping of the Mississippi River and it will flow back upstream. Due to the force of the fault line in this region, there actually might be a new Mountain range that will be higher than the Rocky Mountains.

Similar major Earth Changes will occur on every continent.

There will be terrorist threats in all the major cities. People will want things that they don't deserve and due to anger and greed by all sides we could have Martial Law. We were also warned not to take our freedoms too lightly that they may be physically taken away but to keep strong in spirit.

There will be explosions in buildings in cities across the World. Bridges and tunnels will be collapsing at a terrific rate. Plane crashes and debris from space will cause pain and suffering. Shadows from the dark side will make themselves appear as human and create fear.

New diseases will come to pass and will make AIDS look very harmless.

The monetary system will finally collapse and cause people to be in hysteria. The World Banks will finally cease to exist.

The sun will be causing more forms of skin cancer due to the exposure of ultraviolet light that is no longer deflected.

There could be some visitors of the Extra Terrestrial kind that wouldn't be to our benefit and there could be revealed how the governments of the World have assisted them with experimentation on humans all along.

There will be objects which will be coming towards our Earth. The main function of these objects is to establish order throughout the Galaxies. There are five of them. They are smaller than our moon. However, they are like magnets which are attracted to the opposites. They are focused on Love and when Planets exude love they are shifted away from that planet. However, if the vibration of the planet is negativity, then they move towards the Planet and create balance.

I will not comment any further on this for this is new information. However, I feel that it is important to know that if 10% of humanity is focused in on change and balance and actively working towards enlightenment, then these Master Objects will not affect our Planet and disturb the orbit of the Earth. Also, Michael has said that there may come to pass a Moment when all people will experience a shift in the energies and those people who are not prepared for the change and the wave of Love that will sweep this planet like never before – they will be placed on an Earth that will handle those whose growth has temporarily been stunted and they will learn to grow together.

Again this is a thumb nail sketch of the information that I have received. They have spoken of war in the Middle East, yet there is hope.

So how do the Earth Changes affect us? Every day, we turn on the news and hear about more racial incidents. The use of drugs and violence has increased amongst the youth of the world. Collapses of governments in the Eastern Bloc countries have created a shift in economies and has caused food shortages in those lands. Our water and foods are not safe. We become aware of the environment but what can we do? Jobs are closing down. People are resenting taking care of people who can work but refuse to and say there are no more jobs. Everyone wants everyone else to fix everything around them. We have dysfunctional families and people tell you that you are wrong for getting healthy by not staying in touch with parents, in-laws, grandparents, etc.

So how can it affect you? Many ways. Your first reaction to the changes around you is to run away or reject the
information, feel overwhelmed. If you have a fear response
that is normal. If you have no response, stop reading all
information about Earth Changes and check to see if you
have a pulse.

Recently, I met a woman who said to me that she had read
Beyond A Master and disagreed with what I had written. I said
fine. Yet still she wanted to engage me in conversation. She
stated that she was medically and scientifically based and that
the information was all wrong. I then asked her to explain
the weather and all the unusual things happening today. She
said nothing was strange or unusual about the weather or
anything . . . Many people will not share your view of the
Earth or the Changes, so if you need to talk to someone, go
ahead but understand that unless they are of like mind, they
will rationalize away that the Earth is a limitless resource and
that the world is flat!

So how do you handle your fears about what is happening?
Understand this point of view. All or none of the above may
occur. I will restate what I have announced in the beginning
of all of this: you are responsible for yourself. You must be
able to work on yourself and understand the God energy
within yourself to the best of your ability. You may want
to study the Ancient Truths or study the way of the Native
culture. Whatever you do, do something.

You may find that ancient techniques of meditation and
releasing and letting go are appropriate at this moment in
time. You need to become first whole within, so let us start
with the physical then move to the mental and finally to the
spiritual. Since they are all integrated and go hand in hand
with one another, it is important to know what you can and
cannot do. When you are in tune with yourself, you are in
tune with Nature and will know where to go and where to
be to be safe during this time. Your inner voice will be your
guide and you will meet others who are also working on
themselves. You will be invaluable to one another.

This will also be a sad time for others if spouses or family do not share the views you have. That will be a hard choice to make when the time comes. You must follow your heart no matter what anyone says to you. But, only do those things that you know you can live with for the rest of your lives. Don't leave if you feel that you will be miserable and regret not having your loved one with you.

Simply put, accept yourself and your circumstances for what they are. Do not try to change anyone or anything to have your way. Live your life to the best of your ability and strive for the highest and the best but also acknowledge that at this moment this is **your highest and best**!

So, basically, some Earth Changes are going to happen whether we like them or not. We have put a pendulum into motion and it is in full swing. One or two people can change the course of history, as it has been proven over and over again. But, this time, we are going to awaken as a group. The Coming of Christ is the awakening to the Christ within yourself, the awakening of all the Spirits of the Earth. There is a Bridge between the Native Spirits and the Master Energies like never before on the Earth.

No wonder there is some upheaval! The Earth is cleaning itself out of all the toxins that have been here. As the Guides have been saying for years, if you are sick, you will have a fever, then sweat and sometimes vomit. Before you know it, you are better and such are the Earth Changes on that level. The Earth is going to rid itself of the virus that is making it sick and if it takes a few of the bugs while cleaning out, oh well! When you can see on an overall level that all is as it is meant to be and see it clearly, then you can go on cheerfully with working on your life, knowing full well that everyone is on their Path exactly the way they need to be.

You see, I don't really care if you believe anything that I say. It really is up to Spirit to see that the eyes of those who need this information read it. It is not up to me to try to convince anyone, including family, that the **truth is**. It is always by choice that people will change for their highest and best good. It is not an option for us to feel that we must change all around us. If you take on that job, then you find yourself being pulled down by the undertow of the people around you. You then may lose your footing and the next thing you know, you are just like them, bad mouthing them for not taking the Spiritual Information you have so lovingly offered them. How could they be so blind? When you take on this type of an attitude, you have lost.

This is why, with the Earth Changes, you could point out to someone that the weather is odd, or that there have been an incredible amount of earthquakes, floods, famine, banks collapsing, wars, racial incidents, and so on; and their response might well be 'It's always been like that. It is human nature.' When you receive this response, say nothing if you can. They are blinded to the Truth and, frankly, there isn't that much time left to waste.

So, what other things might you see? Well, according to my Guides, there will be a lot of people dying suddenly. There will be many people taking their own lives as well as unexplainable diseases or just sudden death. This will cause a lot of pain to many people. Even when you understand what death is, it still takes a toll on you. From the spiritual perspective, death is just the continuation of life. What we do here goes into our Akashic Records and plays itself back to us, so that we can see our lessons on Earth and how we best handled them. That is why we work on releasing and letting go here on Earth, so we don't have to go through the heaven and hell states that these emotions evoke – hopefully just the heaven states. When we die, we actually can see those we left behind for 3 to 4 days. Can you imagine all the pain you feel when everyone around the Earth Plane is crying and carrying on? It is a form of selfishness, I am told, that makes us cry out: 'What will I do without them in my life?'

Even with years of study, I too still feel the pain when a friend dies. I believe that this is for most the hardest part of the lessons to learn: that the person is O.K. and in the best place. It truly takes time to heal this. Hopefully, with knowledge of the Path, it takes a bit shorter time to heal than one who does not understand Death.

Besides sudden death, there will be many unpredictable events also occuring to most people on the Earth. But, as I have said, there will be many wonderful things happening. With the availability of the Truth being revealed to all on all things, you can take this one of two ways. You can be horrified to think that someone will know your secret thoughts or you can rejoice in knowing that you are the best that you can be and will learn to accept every single part of yourself as you. You can go about trying to change yourself, but first must appreciate the you that exists at this very moment in time. We are human, therefore we are not Perfect. If you can understand that not one living person on the Earth has ever been born Perfect, then you can start accepting you for you.

So, how do you as an individual handle life today? Are you at this moment regretting you didn't do this or that? Are you sitting smugly saying to yourself: 'Gee! I know all of this already'? Or are you actively engaged in trying to create change in your own personal world, allowing everyone to be who they are? You can do many incredible things to work with the changes. You can start, as I have said before, by taking personal inventory and start blessing all around you. Every time you curse a situation or person, you bring that situation right back to you. Curses, like blessings, are boomerangs. You try to throw it at someone and it will come back to harm you.

With the speeding up of all things around us, you may notice that time is not as stable as it once was. Things are moving so quickly, so get used to it! It will continue to speed up until there will be only the NOW, which is where we are headed, only living in the Present. Those people who are stuck in the past or the future will and may go mad. So be aware that there will be an epidemic of madness all around us.

It is best that you start learning to be self-sufficient and learn to go back to nature. Find out where you truly want to live. There will be many livable places during the more intensified Earth Changes. Remember that our society will be going through a nervous breakdown, so to speak. Living in the cities could prove to be a deadly thing.

With possible shifts of currents in the magnetic fields of the Earth, all engines that work on magnetic fields would temporarily come to a halt. Therefore the more hand-driven or horse-drawn tools and forms of transportation that you have, the better off you are. Even collecting an old fashioned typewriter or two wouldn't be a bad idea. When I say to stock up on seeds, I am not talking about hybrids. Try to find seeds that will reproduce themselves for another crop. Build, starting now, networks with people who know how to do necessary yet almost forgotten skills. Trapping will be necessary. If gasoline is in short supply, then there may be a shortage of meat if that is something that you eat. Learn to fast but in a very positive way. Exercize so that your body is in maximum capacity. If we are to be faced with food shortages, isn't it better to already know how to be healthy and fit with a minimum of food? It is better to be prepared than to find yourself in a fear or panic state. Imagine people in major city areas having to do without food. Can you imagine what they would do? Some would hopefully come together, but the majority might not be so cooperative.

Are you starting to understand the implications of the changes?

Stock up on some basic grains and beans and staples and learn to rotate what you have. Go into a co-op with people whom you trust. This way, you will have a network of food available. Get involved with people who are looking for land. Learn the ways of the land. Farming skills are very necessary as well as learning about herbs and the curative capability of plants. As a Paramedic, as well as a Teacher, I strongly advise some first aid skills or now is the time to become a nurse or Paramedic if you are strongly drawn towards healing, for some of the good old-fashioned physical kind will most definitely be needed. Get away from me with that crystal if someone around me is having a heart attack or medical emergency! Immediate care does take some drastic measures. Then approach me with some calming techniques only after the physical is taken care of.

This is not to say that you cannot combine both forms of healing. I am an advocate of natural healing myself. However, I understand that I am not at this point in my evolution as a human being capable of raising the dead or healing the blind. I am just being honest about my own capability to date. This is extremely important right now to focus in on what skills you have. As they say, go full steam ahead. Now is the time to go to school on any level and learn and learn and learn. Then implement all that you know in your daily life.

Inertia

Eric Morse

Mention the word *inertia* to most people and it will be assumed that we are speaking either of something obscurely mathematical or of that kind of apathy people feel when they just can't stir themselves to do anything. And to some extent I am going to have to talk about both those topics – not because I want to blind us all with science, and certainly not because I want to cast stones at anyone who just doesn't see what they actually **can** do about anything at present. I want to show what Inertia really is, and why it is important to understand how it plays a necessary part in all of us.

If I try to move a heavy object, a garden roller, say, I have to use a lot of sweat and effort just to get it started. But once it is rolling along on a hard smooth surface, I shall have to exert at least as much effort to stop it. My greenhouse wall may stop it before I can!! That is inertia at its most obvious. Scientists say that *a body continues in uniform motion or remains at rest until acted upon by some external force to cause it to do otherwise; and the force required to cause any given rate of change is proportional to the mass of the body and the velocity at which it is moving.* Those are the first two of Isaac Newton's famous laws of Motion, while the third states that *to every action there is an equal and opposite reaction,* i.e. if I try to push the roller forward, it tries to push me back with the same force against me that I am applying against it. That reaction against me is what we call the roller's 'inertia', its inbuilt resistance to being moved. I can only overcome it by digging my feet into the ground, or some such means, which effectively adds a part of Earth's mass to mine, whereas the roller cannot add anything to itself.

We do not need to go further into a physics lesson at this point, until we ask and then answer: What has this to do with Human Development and Evolution?

First of all, what do I mean by those two terms? This is purely arbitrary on my part; by Development, I mean any practice which a human may deliberately undertake to advance its own state in some way, such as seeking education, applying for a better job, learning yoga or jogging to improve the physique – you see the idea, and it is done voluntarily, because he or she wants to do it. By Evolution, I mean a process which is happening to all of us in one way or another, not necessarily all in the same way at the same time, nor at the same rate, but what we all have in common here is that it is happening by the power of some force or command greater than ourselves; it is **not** voluntary on our parts. We have no more choice to argue with it than has the garden roller to argue with me, and most of the time we are scarcely any more conscious of it than is the roller of me.

Development has become very much the 'in thing' over recent years, and in just about every area of our being – physical, mental, emotional, psychic, spiritual, or whatever. The very fact that voluntary Development has indeed become so popular is doubtless in itself an outcome of the involuntary Evolution happening to us, but it is much more with the Evolutionary process on both a personal and a world scale that we shall be concerned with for the rest of my part in this book.

So, having made that distinction clear, where does Inertia come into the matter? It is a phenomenon which is found operating in every arena and at every level of existence in the material world and, as much sound evidence suggests, probably even beyond the material. At the material level we have only to see what happens with something so simple and everyday as the incoming tide. As the wave of deep water enters the shallows, the lower part of it meets with the sand and shingle; the latter resists being moved out of the way and so the energy of the water is taken up with trying to overcome the sand's inertia. The upper part of the water, however, meets with much less resistance from the water beneath it; and so it carries right on its way by its own inertia until, briefly suspended in mid-air, it crashes down in a welter of foam which we call a 'breaker'.

We see the same more dramatically, and happily less often, in the earthquake or the volcanic eruption. A movement in the fluid sub-strata of the Earth comes up against the solid crust which has a very considerable inertia against being moved. At last, however, after much shoving and straining, the fluid wins and the crust cracks. Suddenly the force which has been exerted is far in excess of what is now needed to make a small adjustment to the crust, and the movement goes wildly out of control. The same may happen if my garden roller is initially in a slight rut made by its own weight while standing unused; I apply more force than will be needed once I have got it out of the rut, and it may literally run away with me on a path to disaster.

Both these examples, the everyday tide and the dramatic quake or volcano, are reflected in the Evolution of living creatures – humans no less than any others; indeed probably much more than others. The various adolescent discomforts commonly called 'growing pains' are no more than various parts of the body growing at uneven rates, the faster parts meeting resistance by the slower, and both feeling the ill effects of the contest between their differing inertias.

That is an example at the physical, structural level but we can match it, for example, in the chemical arena. We have within our bodies the chemical factories which we call endocrine glands to produce the various hormones which we shall need later to give us physical strength, defence capabilities, sexual motivation and so on. They are only 'ticking over' at birth but begin their production in earnest at various times throughout our early growth, some not until we reach about seven years, some not until we reach

43

puberty, or even later. As each comes into full operation, its products are almost as foreign to our systems as the contents of some of those bottles which are labelled: *Keep out of reach of children.* We are initially polluted by them, if poisoned be too strong a word for it. Our bodies, our minds, our emotions, possibly our etheric or astral forms too, must adjust to the new chemistry and again there is inertial resistance to be overcome before discomfort ceases and we feel at ease with being different to how we were before.

Such common teenage problems as acne arise from our inertial difficulty in accepting both chemical and bacteriological changes, while the pangs of rising sexual awareness are also the result of hormonal changes making us now need intercourse and exchange with the special energies and qualities of the opposite sex. Prior to these changes we were much more complete – more androgynous, we might almost say – within ourselves. Again, it is inertial resistance to the changes which gives us the problems. (The special problems attending *homosexual* evolution in either sex are a matter of separate study, but again inertia is at the root of the difficulties in coming to terms with it, both in the person concerned and in his/her social and family company.)

The rise of sexual awareness, however, brings us to the verge of another level of evolution and inertial resistance to it, and brings us to begin looking at levels where the effects spread beyond the purely personal arena, all the way through the social, political, ideological and religious battlegrounds, not forgetting the economic.

The fact that our actions in relationship with the opposite sex can now have consequences which were not possible earlier brings us to our first real encounter with moral and ethical problems. We shall usually have had some indoctrination about these matters earlier, but mostly more ethical than moral, and most of it – certainly if the sexual questions were included – seemed remote from anything that was then real to us.

But, those same impulses which in childhood days caused

us quite innocently to put our arms around another child or adult as an expression of love and affection suddenly assume a different quality which may lead to them being resented or repelled by the recipient, and they may well be condemned by the onlookers as indecent assault. The giver of the embrace will be just as much aware as the receiver that he/she now feels some new, extra motive in it, something which causes uncertainty and inhibition – guilt too, if the action has been repelled, or criticised by parent, priest, teacher or passing busybody – and yet the inertia of the previous, pre-pubertic state still protests that no harm is meant, while the chemistry of the new state cannot understand why it should be denied the exercise that it is so obviously intended for.

The owner of the body thus afflicted must learn, much too fast for comfort, to harmonise the inertia of the old state with that of the new one; and although the higher energy centres most actively engaged are those of the feelings and emotions, the adjustment must be undertaken in the intellectual centres before the other two can be brought into line. The intellectual centres can rationalise and present a case; the emotions and feelings can but simply act. All too often they are forced into obedience by dictatorial suppression – repression if you prefer to call it that – and the resultant damage can be anything from life-long guilt complexes, through bitter antisocial behaviour, to such painful and ultimately fatal physical ills as cancer, motor neurone disorders, Parkinson's disease and much, much more. A large range of lesser but almost equally disabling physical complaints have the same inertial conflicts at the root of them. Smoothing out the 'breakers' of the oncoming tide of puberty is still one of the least successfully handled matters of our health.

The medical profession spends much effort in discussing whether an individual's problems, physical and/or psychological, have set in at some particular point during the life, or whether they are congenital – i.e.: he was born with it – but we have good reason for saying that the seeds of the main disorders in us are sown as far back as the moment of our conception. Our existence begins there in a very brief moment of activity, but an enormous amount happens then. Shortly before it our parents couple together and place in the womb tiny seeds which, just like today's micro-chips in computers, contain what to the layman is an incredible amount of information, all taken from 'the state of the art', from the past up to that moment, and setting the pattern of how the product, computer or human, will work throughout its lifespan. In fact the human sperm and ovum contain far more than any silicon chip, and computer technologists have recognised this and experimented with chips of living protein in an attempt to match the natural capacity for storing and passing on information on such a huge scale.

What is actually happening at this conception? Where does it fit into our discussion of human evolution?

The new life is taking on board everything that is present, everything that has been experienced in the lives and stored in the memories, conscious and unconscious, of the two parents. We can mention their physical conditions of health, their psychological states, their knowledge, understanding and beliefs springing from what has been taught to them, and any kinds of neuroses that have scarred them as a result of accidents and other fears, worries and sufferings they have endured. We must not leave out, of course, all their happy experiences and the conclusions they have drawn from those.

In addition to all that, there must be the contents of what each of the parents in their turn inherited in the same way during their own conceptions from their parents. In general, those contents should be a little weaker than what they transmit from their own life experiences, but we certainly must not write them off. If a grandparent has undergone some very significant experience, something traumatic, or a serious illness, or has held some important position in the community – to give just a few examples – then that will have introduced a new piece of 'coding' into the family memory-bank which may well continue to make itself felt through several generations to come. As the examples show, the effect may be felt in the physical, psychological or cultural levels in us, or in any combination of them. That this effect

46

over several generations has been known for a long time is confirmed when we read, in the Bible, of God *visiting the iniquity of the fathers upon the children, and upon the children's children unto the third and fourth generation.* (Exodus, 34, vii). The book might better have said *inequity* or *imbalance* to express what is really at work here; the judgemental moralism of the word actually in the Bible may stem from the ignorance of the original writer, or that of later translators.

The extent of that kind of inheritance may well be much more than four generations in certain extreme cases and in respect of a family line having come almost unaltered down centuries along just one very strongly imposed cultural pattern. People who have undergone past-life regression therapy under hypnosis have reported traumas and guilt complexes going back hundreds of years through either their own past lives or the lives of their ancestors, or both, depending upon the belief system one uses to assess such reports. The important thing is that the reports are valid and genuine *in all cases where distress is still being felt*, no matter what doubts some of our analysts may express about them. Were they not valid at some level or other in the patient, the distress would not now be present. It should also be remarked here, by the way, that this same factor of heavy traumas in the past accounts for why it is that people who recall past lives never seem to have been 'just ordinary' people; something special seems always to have happened to them. The simple fact is that they do not remember matters which leave no impact, only the great or traumatic events, whether in their own lives or in lives of their ancestors, whichever way we like to explain their memories.

The matter of cultural inheritance, which shows up mostly in religious and moral allegiance, is something which will come up several times yet as we continue this understanding of ourselves. For now, it is enough to remark that, positively, it often acts as an anchor by which we retain a measure of stability and assurance during times of trouble and confusion around us: 'If you can keep your head when all around you, are losing theirs . . .' as Kipling put it. We go on believing, or at least hoping with just a tinge of belief, that God as we have been taught about Him is watching what goes on and will bring matters out to the right conclusion.

That much is fine for much of the time, but the negative side is that 'God as we have been taught about Him' is very far short of the Real Intelligence which governs our world, and that a very large part and cause of our troubles stems straight from our clinging to concepts of God which simply have not expanded to cope with the world as it is now – a world vastly changed from how it was in the days of Moses, Buddha, Jesus and even the lattermost of the great prophets, Muhammad – and presumably changed because God has willed it to change. At least no-one who believes God to be Omnipotent can suppose that any change has happened which He has not willed or permitted!

So we are beginning to get a clear picture of this inertia, this built-in resistance within each of us, founded on that same universal principle of Inertia as Newton discovered it in the simple arena of mechanics. *It keeps us on a steady course, holding us together when we should otherwise fly apart at random in all directions; yet it also gives us pain, distress and sickness as we try to keep pace with the evolution going on all the time within us* – an evolution of whose nature and many levels of working we are still almost entirely ignorant – and more ignorant than we now should be. We have scarcely ever troubled even to consider our evolution from here onwards as a subject for investigation, notwithstanding the fortunes we have spent on exploring its past ever since Darwin excited us about it.

So, while in this present chapter we have so far talked only of those evolutions which happen to us as part of our 'normal' growing process, into the seemingly familiar and well understood creature that our species already is, it must now be clear that our species – and every one of us personally as part of it – is also the target and vehicle of further evolutionary processes of which as yet we know almost nothing. We may give ourselves a little pat on the back for being probably the first species ever to be even postulating and asking about such processes. But we are having great difficulty, for all that, in adjusting smoothly to what is happening to us.

2

Human Evolution

In The Beginning!

Eric Morse

In religious language, the Lord our God is working some
great miracle in us, but we are not attentive to His instructions, and we are resisting what He is doing, so we are
suffering for our **Sin**!!! That is meant to be taken with a
smile or two, if you can manage it in all your trials, yet it
is also a statement of a profound truth if it be understood
rightly.

The word *Sin* has nothing to do fundamentally with
being a bad boy or girl, though religion has preached it that
way for a very long time now. It actually springs from an
ancient word meaning to be *separated* or *cut off* from the larger
unit or body of which one has hitherto been an integral part.
That state may be of one's own choosing, in which case any
ill effects are surely to be laid upon one's own head, as also
any benefits gained if the separation is, say, independence
from some foreign imperial rule. The Irish political party
Sinn Fein derives its name from the same root as *Sin* and
was of course formed to gain independence for Ireland from
Britain. *Mount Sinai* likewise derives its name from its lonely
position in the desert.

But Sin as we are speaking of it here is a clinical mal-
function of our nervous system – just that, and nothing to
do with being naughty or irreligious except insofar as those
phenomena are the results of the clinical condition, not its
cause.

The nub of the matter is, some twelve thousand years ago, a catastrophic star explosion perilously close to Earth brought about a massive irradiation of the planet and most of its life forms were annihilated almost overnight. This is the explanation of the skeletal remains of herds of dinosaur found in Colorado, and of the frozen bodies of similar herds of mammoth in Siberia, many with the grass on which they were feeding still in their mouths, apparently struck down en masse without warning. The very sudden appearance of a new species of Man, Cromagnon Man, which has baffled scientists for so long, is also a part of this same event. The author Stanley Gooch has written much about the biology of this matter, while Otto Muck, Jack Countryman, Santillana & von Dechend, and the present writer, to mention but a few names, have covered the history of the event. The most relevant works are listed in the bibliography to this volume.

The remnants of life that survived the *catastrophe* – the very word means loss of a star, as also does the word *disaster* – suffered a cancerous outgrowth of the brain material with the result that a new brain system, only poorly connected to the old one, was created. The old brain is what we now call the *cerebellum*, whose functioning is still only sketchily understood by today's experts in neurology, while the new growth includes all of the much larger structure, midbrain, hypothalamus, neo-cortex – all that we now speak of as being 'The Brain', assuming as we do that the old cerebellum just runs the automatic workings in us.

That is the situation in most forms of mammal life today, though it has reached its extreme in Man, whose high-domed skull is the mark of the expansion that made such a skull necessary. Other creatures closely related to us have much flatter skulls, containing less of the new growth and indicating that either they dwelt in places more protected from the radiation or that their survival was less successful than ours, with probable degeneration from what they had been before, rather than the expansive evolution that happened to us.

We are mainly concerned here with our own species,

54

however, and with how we stand today in the aftermath of that evolutionary leap which happened, not millions of years ago but only just at the edge of our recorded history. It is important that we understand that a) the leap was comparatively recent, contrary to expert opinions considered sacrosanct from the time of Darwin until only a few years ago, and b) that leap did not mark the end of our evolution, as again expert opinion tended to assume, but the evolution is still going ahead and is very close indeed to yet another major leap.

Our present situation, then, is one of a serious cleft between the old and new brains, the Cerebellum and the much larger assembly which we commonly call 'The Brain', in consequence of which each is markedly ignorant of what the other thinks and does, or how it thinks and does it. Read almost any book about the brain and we find much discussion about the respective functions of the Right and Left Hemispheres, but no mention at all of the connections and relationship with the Cerebellum. That tightly compacted unit just above the top end of the spinal column is correctly guessed – rather than precisely known – to keep a controlling watch of some kind over how our body is functioning; and it is now realised that, small though it is in volume, it is actually larger in number of cells than the Cortex, so tightly is it now compressed beneath a skull that was once all its own. Beyond that limited knowledge of it, the Cerebellum is as mysterious and remote to us as all our guesswork about God.

I chose my words carefully there. A very considerable part of what we believe to be commandments issuing from the Deity are actually instructions coming over very tenuous communication lines from that old brain unit to the new one. We have great difficulty in understanding what it delivers because it has a very different pattern of thought and perception to the Cortex, especially to the latter's Left Hemisphere's simplistic 'digital' mode of working – arithmetical, grammatical, logical, rational – and it seems that communication at all is only possible through the Right Hemisphere's capacity for a more imaginative way of working – intuition, 'getting the picture', feeling rather than calculating the message in precise detail.

If that is how things look from the standpoint of the Cortex, it is not much easier from the Cerebellum's end of the line. Current knowledge of the nerve connections indicate that the Cerebellum is blind, having no direct connection to our eyesight, so that its knowledge of the visible world about us must be conveyed to it through the image-making ability of the cortical Right Hemisphere, much as one might describe something to a person who had sight a long time ago but has been struck blind by injury in early youth. The Cerebellum does seem to have access to our hearing, however, and has shown signs in experiments that it responds more readily to 'prayers' spoken aloud than to those merely thought in silence. It also has the ability to register very subtle taste stimuli and to respond to them, which is probably why homeopathy works: Gross doses of poison register so strongly with the Cortex that the Cerebellum is unable to intervene against its big brother's clumsy handling of the situation, but microscopic doses escape the notice of the Cortex and leave the old brain free to act correctly upon the hint it has thus received.

Yet another capacity of the Cerebellum would seem to be its ability to over-ride our habitual sense of Time, for it seems most likely that it is the old brain which gives us those glimpses into the future which we call clairvoyance, or at least which registers them and passes them on from whatever source it itself receives them. There is much yet to be researched in that particular matter, and we shall touch upon it again ourselves in my final chapter. Suffice it to say for the moment that clairvoyance and foreknowledge of the future are not suspect rarities found in only a few 'mediumistic' people, they were proven long since to be a commonplace part of the nocturnal dreaming of every one of us, as J. W. Dunne showed in 'An Experiment with Time', as important a book as has yet been written this century.

There we have a useable sketch, then, of the most vital part of our present make-up – useable to explore further both this matter of our in-built inertia, and also the thorny, much misconstrued phenomenon which we term Sin. We can see now that what our religions call Sin, (implying in the same breath that it is something which is our personal fault, and for which we shall be condemned unless we repent and behave according to their prescribed dogmas for our salvation), is precisely and only that state of separation, of cut-offness, of almost no clear and intelligible contact between that original brain that we call the Cerebellum and the more recent out-growth that we call the Cortex, or just 'The Brain'. I cannot say that I have yet seen any religion teach this actual truth of the situation.

Yet it is just the struggle to repair that brain damage that all religious urging and counselling to hear and obey the 'Word of God' is aiming at, albeit *knowing not what they do*! Religion's struggle is hamstrung from the outset by its abysmal ignorance of what and where the damage really is. Centuries of *learned* debate about whether or not the immortal soul can sin and, if not, then what part of us can and does sin, have gone hand-in-hand along with mystifying copies of magical rituals whose original meaning and correct conduct have been forgotten, or deemed unsafe for us common people to know them.

Yet every situation, even the worst and most hopeless, can have its benefic outcome and of course we have learned much indeed at many levels or planes of life from our experiments conducted in ignorance, even if we have to say that more was learned by 'lucky accident' than by skilled intention. Very slowly at first, and with far too many good enquirers beheaded or burned alive for their courage, we have learned more and more about ourselves and our world and universe; and the inertia represented by the conservatism of religion has not universally always been a bad thing. Its reminder that we are part and parcel of something greater than just ourselves, something greater indeed than just the universe our eyes and telescopes can see, has often been an inspiration rather than a fetter to our enquirers, and a brake to keep us moving forward at a pace we could feel comfortable with, at least until religion and science separated onto almost irreconcilable platforms around the end of the last century.

The consequences of that split are discussed more later, along with the reasons for it. At the moment, it is enough to say that while, undoubtedly, it spurred us into an unprecedented leap in science at the technological level, and thus made possible our present capacity to understand ourselves in quite new ways, at the same time we now had two schools in place of the previous one, each asserting the ultimate knowledge of all things, and each cultivating a perversely deliberate, and aggressively deliberate, ignorance of what the other had to offer.

Ignorance, deliberate or innocent, must no longer be our way forward. For, while the unseen finger guiding us from behind it has eventually led us to some glimpses of a higher knowledge, the ignorance itself has also led us into the peril which we find ourselves and our planet in today, a peril which the gloomier amongst us feel well justified in seeing as the possibility of our utter extinction, so that further dabbling with ignorance is a luxury we can no longer afford.

What we have just encountered and analysed, then, is that working of inertia which I mentioned earlier at the long-entrenched cultural level in us. It keeps us firmly attached to what we have known, or believed we knew in the past, and it takes us much time, effort and even pain to overcome that inertial attachment, even when we know it is no longer valid. I well recall my own mother still pricing everything in pounds, shillings and pence to the end of her days, sixteen years after Britain's decimalisation of its currency. At least our currency never had the aura of God's Will upon it or we might not, any of us, have adjusted to the change yet! Where religion has had a hand in our conditioning our struggle to move forward is hardest of all – even though the advance may well be, almost certainly **is** what the Divine Intelligence truly wills for us.

No religion is exempt from that verdict, yet neither should any be blamed on account of it. They have struggled with the same clinical disability that is in all of us, and with only the same ignorance, not greater than in the rest of us, of its true nature. And if the religious have often postulated ridiculous answers to a problem they have not even suspected to exist, the materialists have usually done even worse. They have insisted complacently that there is neither any problem in the first place, nor any way forward at all except by the vagaries of what they have preached to be a meaningless, accidental universe of matter, and nothing more than that. At least the angels guiding the religious have managed now and then to get some little snippet of the true wonder of *The Intelligent Universe* through to them. That phrase in italics, by the way, is the title of one of the books by the astronomer Sir Fred Hoyle, and an excellent guide it is for anyone with a mind slightly attuned to science, wanting an exhilarating view of where the Universe is taking us. Clearly, angels do not limit their counsel just to those who preach in places of worship.

The way forward, then, must be to rely only on what we truly know, but always with an abiding Faith that we shall yet be shown more of what we still need to know, for there will always be an infinite mountain of wisdom greater than what we yet have. Our knowledge has been described as a growing disc of light in a field of infinite darkness: the bigger the circle gets, the longer becomes the perimeter that measures what as yet we do **not** know. Still hiding within that infinity is much that will challenge and then overthrow what we have believed we knew until now, and we must learn to recognise when it is time to make the change in our knowledge and in ourselves. The whole reason why we inherit all that we take on board at our conception is that we bring it into new times, new conditions, a new stage in Evolution, and we replant only so much of it as will grow to health and splendour in the new season, blending it with what we newly discover, but not trying to replant those things which were never meant to outlast their one season.

Something more of what we shall yet find within the vast unknown around us – and within us – is my topic for the final chapter in this section, where I want to speak among other things about planes of life, other worlds as we are accustomed to call them, of which we are still woefully ignorant but of which we most surely are going to know much more within the next very few years. Again, we shall find that we have to revise, even discard as erroneous, much that we believe we know today, and we shall do well to be brave and echo the words of the humourist Josh Billings: '*It ain't what a man* **don't** *know as makes him a fool, but what he* **does** *know as* **ain't so**!'

The Fall From Unity

Nick Bamforth

In order to understand how humanity has got itself into this present state of crisis, it is important to go back into our evolution and discover the forces which have made us into the kind of creatures we have become.[1]

In looking back to the early part of our evolution, and also in comparing 'modern man' to the so-called primitive societies which still exist today, we tend to arrogantly presume that we are superior to them. We judge them from our 'sophisticated' rational standpoint and see them in terms of the material and technological world which we have created.

What we must understand about early man is that he or she (I apologize about the continuous use of he, but do so for ease of expression!) was essentially an intuitive creature, whose survival was dependant on the survival of the group, just as we see with most primates today. The group and the immediate environment were the essential reality and the individuals were bound together by what I term the Universal Authority of the Group – an innate feeling of connection not only between the individual members of the group, but also with the Earth and a greater Whole.

What set us apart from other animals was that spark which evolved into what we now term as the rational mind,

[1]For a more comprehensive investigation of this, please refer to my book *Duality into Unity* published in 1992.

but what I like to call in these early stages the sequential mind. In addition to the intuitive connection to the Whole, man gradually found that he had the ability to discern individual elements of this whole and create things out of them, one creation following in sequence from another. Once initiated, this process became like a steam roller, forging inexorably onwards flattening everything in its path.

Of course, this began very slowly, developing within the confines of the Universal Authority of the Group over thousands of years. The ability to make simple tools and communicate with a verbal language, rather than the many other means of communication which we have since lost, were the two major facets of this new part of us which enabled us to add two things together in a creative way; yet, initially, this did not disturb the essential unity of the group or extended family unit.

Within this unity, there was an innate sense of the continuity of life, even after death – an acceptance of which is necessary for us to understand the rituals of earlier cultures. The earliest evidence of ritual goes as far back as Neanderthal man, who buried their dead along an east-west axis with supplies to help them on their new journey. In the early hunter/gatherer groups, as with the few that still exist today, the frenzied dancing and singing which would precede the hunt was a means of entering a deeper state of communion with the spirits of nature which we cannot perceive with our senses and with the spirit of the animal which was to give its life to nourish others. (All of this may seem a load of superstitious hocus-pocus to modern man, but compare this mutual respect between hunter and prey with our inhumane factory farming, the end product of which most of us consume while not even acknowledging that an animal has given its life so that we can live.)

The simple cohesive unit of the hunter/gatherer group endured almost unchanged for thousands of years and it is within its framework that the sequential mind established itself and grew. However, within an essentially nomadic and tightly knit community, its true power could never be fully unleashed, for the very structure which nurtured it also constrained its growth. It is only with the permanent settling of man, following his discovery of how to cultivate plants, that the sequential mind came into its own.

Those first agricultural communities have been represented as a true Garden of Eden in mythology throughout the world. No longer was there such a hard struggle to survive as there had been before and yet there still remained the harmonious bonding of the group. Within this group, woman had not yet become the secondary figure of later cultures. In many ways, she was now the focal point of the group, as, in the earlier hunter/gatherer groups, it had been she who had gathered the fruits of the earth while man had gone out to hunt. It was she who understood the mysterious life cycles of the Earth and the respect for her powers can be seen from the many female goddess figurines which date from this period.

This initial balance of the female reaper and the male herder, depicted in the universal myths of the Earth Goddess reigning together with her male consort the Bull, was perhaps one of the final moments of true harmony in the evolution of man, for it is not long before man and the divisive, rational mind begin to gain supremacy over woman and over the intuitive harmony which reigned not only within the group, but also with the Earth and with a deeper reality. As civilization 'advances', female energy, associated not only with the mysterious, changing currents of the moon and the Earth but also with the equally powerful force of sexual creativity, gradually comes to be perceived as something dangerous, a threat to the new order of male domination, represented by the shining light of the sun.

What contributed most strongly to this change was the growth in population and in material possessions resulting from the relative ease of this new, settled life. As population grew and as verbal language and division of labor became more complex, differences between individuals became more sharply delineated and consciousness of 'self' became imprinted within the psyche of man.

Much has been written about the so-called 'selfish nature' of man, but the self-interest which is inherent within all of us is no more than an extension of our instinct for survival. When the Universal Authority is invested within the group, all relates to the survival of the group; when this Authority begins to crumble and is transferred to a family unit and then increasingly to the individual, the survival instinct evolves into family- or self-interest. This is a natural evolutionary process; the negative association we feel towards the term self-interest arises from the opposite state from the Universal Authority of the Group, when self-interest is not counterbalanced by an inherent feeling for the larger group of humanity.

As population expanded and communities became larger, the Universal Authority of the Group gradually lost its power and a new hierarchy of intelligence became established. In an animal group, power is most often dependent on physical strength, and there is a continuous process of renewal as the strength of one dominant member fades and is replaced by new, younger blood. The world of intelligence and self-awareness is, however, one of inequality. There are certain people who become more useful than others within the group (i.e. making the best use of their new rational faculties), and, presumably, these were the ones who built around them a new hierarchy of power which was ultimately passed down and kept within the confines of a specific unit within the extended community.

Possessions are an important adjunct of intelligence. First of all, they are a result of man's creative, sequential mind, and, at the same time, they delineate inequality in easily perceivable terms. From the moment man settles in one place, begins to build houses and accumulate things around him, possessions become the symbols of success and power. If we combine this with the inequality of this new world of intelligence, as well as the innate drive within man to improve his material condition and the competition caused by man's increasing population, the perpetual conflict which is the hallmark of our history can be seen as an understandable progression in our evolution. As the spiritual, connective essence of man's being fades, the temporal material world takes over and possession becomes the stimulus and the reward of power.

The growth of individual consciousness, inequality and material possessions are thus inextricably linked together from the very beginning of our evolution and therefore cannot be judged as the 'root of all evil'. When we view them in a negative light, we see individual consciousness in terms of ego, which we can judge as being the root of selfishness, pride, competitiveness and intolerance; we see inequality in terms of the exploitation of the weak by the powerful, of the rich by the poor; we see the pollution and terrible state of our environment as being the result of our obsession with material prosperity at all costs.

What we must understand, though, is that these 'negative' associations have arisen quite simply because these aspects of our evolution have not been nurtured within an environment where the connection between all beings and with the Source of our Being is innately felt. Our awareness of self is what enables us to expand our experience and consciousness, so that we can use our free will to act with responsibility and individual conscience; inequality is part of the diversity of such a world and our responsibility is to use our individual talents for the good of the Whole; our material achievements are a result of great human creativity, and our responsibility is not allowing destruction to be a result of this creativity.

Only when we reach the point of accepting these aspects of our evolution without judgment, trusting our conscience and living with a natural expression of love for one's fellow man – only then will we be on the path towards creating the kind of world most of us, deep down, wish to see.

One of the great leaps in human evolution took place with the appearance of the first large city states in the Middle East around 3500 B.C. There no longer existed within them the intimate connection between the group as a whole and the Earth and Universal Energy; instead, a new, hereditary, priestly hierarchy had arisen to act as an intermediary between the individuals of the community and this Universal Energy which was symbolized as the Great Goddess of infinite space and interpreted through the movement of the stars and planets in the night sky.

At this point of man's evolution, out of seemingly nowhere, there appeared what we consider to be the earliest hallmarks of civilization as we know it: writing, mathematics, astronomy, architecture on a grand scale, the wheel, a system of taxation, and many others. It was the beginning of the new order where the rational mind came to dominate the intuitive connection to the Whole and where man gained ascendancy over woman. In ancient mythology, the female has always symbolized the expansive nature of the Universe beyond the rational understanding of man, yet, from this point on, it is the male principle which predominates, giving form to the world around us and dividing this limitless Universe into parts to which we can relate.

Whereas this process is the essence of our evolution into the dominant species on this planet, it was not gained without cost to the human psyche. The greater the triumphs of the rational mind, the further man was swept away from his past sense of unity with his immediate environment and with the Whole, the Source of his Being. While many cultures, especially such as Ancient Egypt and those of the East, retained a sense of connection to the Whole and a firm belief in the eternity of life beyond physical death, those which created the foundation of our Western civilization were subject to the ultimate crisis of duality: the conscious mind, which followed its innate drive forwards to explore and create the 'best' reality on the physical plane, struggling with the subconscious longing to return to unity with the Whole and with the fear engendered by the loneliness of this separation.

This fear and sense of separation pervades the Semitic Creation myth of Adam and Eve, later assumed by the Christian Church. There are three elements which stand out in this story: first of all, it is an external God who creates Man; then, it is this same external Being who creates Woman out of a part of Man; and, finally, it is Woman who, tempted by the evil Serpent, is responsible for the Fall – a reflection of the extent to which the female creative power had been debased and suppressed by the time this myth came to be written down.

This is in stark contrast with the Hindu and other Eastern traditions where God just was. Only when he articulated the word 'I' and thereby formulated a consciousness of self does he feel that he is alone. So, in order to fill this loneliness, it is he who splits himself in two and makes woman out of himself. Then, in uniting with his other half, he creates mankind.

In the Garden of Eden, man is created, then woman and there is harmony followed by the Fall. After the Fall, Adam and Eve are driven out of the Garden by the curses of this relentless, external God, and flee not only in fear, but also weighed down by the burden of **guilt** for having done wrong, for having 'sinned'. The extent of this fear, combined with the weight of guilt, is the hallmark of the Judaic/Christian mentality.

In the Eastern tradition, it is the very act of Creation, of creating two out of one, which could be interpreted as the Fall, as this represents a division of the energy of One, so that the figure of One, of God, of the Whole, multiplies and fragments into many pieces. And, yet, it is not a Fall at all, as it is all part of the plan, the will to expand and to experience brought to fruition by the Self, rather than by an outside force.

Furthermore, the Old Testament story is the only one in which the serpent is a source of what is judged as evil. In all other spiritual traditions of the world, it represents duality in its most creative aspects of knowledge, consciousness and sexuality: Buddha was protected by a great Serpent King while he sat under the Bodhi Tree – a representation of the universal image of the Cosmic Tree, which, with the serpent wrapped around it, unites the physical world below to the spiritual dimension above; the caduceus of Hermes, the Greek god of mystic knowledge and rebirth, consists of two copulating snakes entwined along a staff; even in the Levant, thousands of years before the Book of Genesis was written, the serpent was worshipped as a deity in its own right. The list is endless.

The serpent, regularly shedding its skin with a new one beneath it, is also the symbol of rebirth and the eternal cycles of life, including the female menstrual cycle, and this idea runs counter to the Judaic idea of an all male, external God, Yahweh, which rules over man. In this new religion, gone is the idea of the individual's connection to the Whole and a cyclical view of the Universe; instead, there comes into being an ethic which has more to do with maintaining order within a specific racial culture in an era of turmoil than bringing man closer to his spiritual nature. The energy of the individual, unleashed from the natural restraint of the Universal Authority of the Group, is perceived as a threat to this order and therefore laws, supposedly of divine origin, are imposed as an artificial restraint.

The guilt, fear and notion of sin inherent in the Judaic, Christian and the related Islamic mentality lie at the heart of much of the confusion and emptiness which exists within our contemporary society. Scratch beneath the surface of many Western men and women and you will find a deep-rooted lack of self-worth which drives us forward to prove ourselves in the eyes of others and set ourselves goals directed more towards external appearance or prosperity rather than the fulfilment of our own inner being. The fear of failure or of being judged for contravening 'moral' standards imposed by a rigid, prohibitive society suppresses the creative energy of our free, individual natures.

The fear of the unruly power of the individual is comprehensible when one considers the immense turmoil which occurred throughout the area of the 'cradle of civilization' after the great city-states disintegrated. Unleashed from the Universal Authority of the Group, individuals and races migrated in every direction, both physically and symbolically, causing chaos and conflict in their path for hundreds of years as they continuously collided with each other. It is hardly surprising that the new hierarchies which finally predominated should make sure that their top priority was the maintenance of order and the resulting suppression of individual expression.

What we fail to understand today is that the seemingly immutable laws of government, society and organized religion are a direct result of the fear of the power of the individual which arose in this period and was reinforced in the Middle Ages and other later periods of apparent chaos. Once more, we have allowed this rigidity to rule our lives rather than understanding that it is the individual's inability to feel his connection to his fellow man and to the greater Whole which brought about the need to impose these so-called 'righteous' laws in the first place. Accepting these ancient 'moral' precepts as absolute truths relevant in today's world has led us to the crisis point we find ourselves facing today. It is only by overcoming the guilt and fear of our own nature that we will learn to trust our intuition and create a world built on the common binding force of Love which is within all of us – something which will only occur once the old hierarchies of power and control have worn themselves out and collapsed.

The ancient Greek civilization, which reached its height around 500 B.C. and which initially felt no such need to suppress the individual, represents another pivotal point in our evolution, laying the foundations for what we now perceive as the mentality of Western man. By bringing man (this excludes woman who was definitely a second-class citizen) to the center of the stage, the individual's responsibility was to actively participate in every aspect of the running of the community or 'polis'. The role of religion diminished as men focused their minds on finding a rational explanation to the Universe rather than feeling an intimate connection to It.

Thales of Miletus is the first man accredited with the question: 'What is the Earth made of?' This first attempt to understand the Universe in human, material terms spawned generations of philosophers and set man on a path of rational enquiry which continues to this day. Yet, in its early days, philosophical thought was still bound in with a sense of awe and connection to the Whole. The great philosopher and mathematician, Pythagoras, was deeply influenced by the secret teachings of the Egyptian Mystery Schools, and, within his belief in reincarnation and purification of the soul, philosophical enquiry was, for him, the only way for the soul to transcend physical reality. His quest was for the first cause and principle of all things, and he saw this as being Number – not in terms of his mathematical laws which are taught to us in school, but as a Universal Principle of Order which lies behind all things, embodied by such universal numbers as π and ϕ as well as by the natural harmonic principles within music.

The separation of rational thought from a broader spiritual sense of the Whole would have been alien to Pythagoras, but, in seeing the rational, immaterial soul as being distinct from and superior to the 'defective' world of the senses, he promoted a separation between the body and the mind/soul, as opposed to the Egyptian view of the body as the 'Temple of the Spirit'. Such distinctions between supposed opposites became a more and more common feature of rational thought, as man tried to make sense of the world around him. The result was a greater understanding of the material principles behind our physical world coupled with an increasing separation from any natural sense of unity with the Whole.

This was particularly true of the two giant philosophers, Plato and Aristotle, who had perhaps the greatest influence of any individuals over the development of Western mentality. They lived at a time when the great Athenian ideal of individual responsibility and communal participation was degenerating, and they were therefore driven by the need to create some sense of rationally comprehensible order out of the apparent disorder around them. Although this was their aim, the result of their searching was quite the contrary.

Plato, like Pythagoras, tried to find an explainable essence within all things. However, whereas Pythagoras saw numb-ber as an expression of the harmony of some deeper reality, Plato's Theory of Forms places the rational quite firmly over the material with minimal emphasis on any force beyond the rational, leading to an essential division between body, mind and spirit. What is more, his need to see the world in rationally comprehensible terms destroyed the validity of a more fluid world dependent on subjective, personal judgment. This was certainly not his intention, but he opened the way for those who later wished to impose on others their own rigid, 'moral' idea of what is right and what is wrong – in particular, in this new world of separation of body, mind and spirit, for those who wished to use the 'higher authority' of an external God to suppress all that pertained to individual, spiritual quest or to the world of the senses.

Plato's great body of work shows how he took upon himself the heavy burden of responsibility to try to create a just society, yet he unwittingly led Western man further away from this ideal. What he could not understand was that he was part of an evolutionary force which was far beyond his control; he could not have forseen how his genuine attempt to create a just society based on mutual respect would be perverted by those whose sole interest was their own power.

His former pupil, Aristotle, continued this process even further. In his 'Metaphysics', he once more tries to delve into the motivating force behind Creation and comes up with the concept of an immovable mover which he humanizes in a way more similar to the God of the Jews than the abstract ideal of the Good put forward by Socrates and Plato. In his famous treatises on logic, he puts forward a system of totally rational thought with the supposed absolutes of truth and falsehood leaving no room for the shades of grey in the middle. In his search for 'eudaimonia' – the material well-being and happiness of man – he abandons his predecessors' quest for a higher reality, whether of a spiritual or rational nature, and focuses his rational powers quite solidly on the material plane.

His is the first truly influential materialist ethic, and, what is more, he turns his back on the former ideal of individual expression with his strongly expressed belief that the good of the individual should always submit to the good, and in particular the order, of the 'polis' or state – even, in his own words, if this is a 'bad' state.

Aristotle was once the tutor of Alexander the Great whose amazing conquests lay the foundations for the rise of the large scale state. Alexander died in 323 B.C. and Aristotle died the following year, ushering in the death of both the political and philosophical ideals of the earlier Golden Age. From now on, all Greek thought centred around such self-centred 'philosophies' as Scepticism and Epicureanism, the aims of which were to find personal peace of mind and pleasure, dismissing any pretension of concern for one's fellow men. On the political plane, power passed to the institutionalized State of Rome.

The world into which Christ was born was a Judaic culture, increasingly influenced by Greek (Hellenistic) rational thought and under the dominion of Roman might where all was subordinate to the State. Within three hundred years after the death of Jesus, the Christ Consciousness had been so deeply submerged under the weight of those three powerful forces of Judaism, Greek thought and the Roman State that the religion which came to bear Christ's name had more in common with them than with the Christ Consciousness itself.

When Emperor Constantine espoused Christianity for political reasons and imposed his authority on its teachings at the Council of Nicaea in 325 A.D., the essence of Christ's teachings of Love, the God Within and the temporal nature of the material world were finally supressed – something which centuries of earlier persecution had failed to do. Where Christ had taught humility and surrender and had renounced the trappings of the material world, Christianity's new champion raised himself up as the great warrior, killing the enemies of a God which was now made manifest in imperial power and wealth.

When Constantine died and the Roman Empire declined, the Christian Church itself assumed the Roman Imperial colours and began to imitate the State in every way, living in palaces, raising armies and assuming wealth and property as its right. It promoted the Judaic concept of an external, male, vengeful God which handed down a set of immutable, social laws; it became obsessed with theological argument as to the nature of God; and, where Christ brought spiritual consciousness out of the temple into the lives of the common people, Christianity squeezed it back into the confines of the Church, ruthlessly persecuting as heresy any individual quest for a return to the Unity of the Whole.

The thousand years that followed in the West were marked by the continuous battle for material supremacy between Church and State, which differed very little from each other in their thirst for power and rigid control of the masses. Yet in the North, where Roman influence was only fleeting, the old 'pagan' religions endured much more strongly, even after Christianity had been adopted as the official, 'exclusive' religion. Far from being the mere superstition of primitive heathens, these native religions were much closer to a sense of Unity with the Earth and the Universe than the monolithic religion which tried to suppress them. There had existed a distinct civilization long before the arrival of the Romans – Stonehenge, for example, was one of many stone circles in Britain, Ireland and Northern Europe which were built in alignment with the movement of the sun and the moon and where ritual, coinciding with the passages of the seasons, was presided over by a priesthood which was responsible for maintaining harmony between its community and Nature, the Earth and the Universe.

This pagan spirit which saw a natural harmony and order in Nature and beyond exists to a degree today in such cultures as the Native Americans and Australian Aboriginals, as well as many of the so-called 'primitive' cultures around the world. We would do well to return to the teachings of these native traditions; they have been handed down for centuries to the few who have kept them in safe keeping, until man reaches that point when he is ready to tap into the power of the elemental energies of the Earth for the good of the whole rather than for his own upliftment.

We have of course still not reached that point. At the end of the Middle Ages, when the old order of power crumbled, any movement towards a more personal, spiritual quest was quickly buried beneath another emerging force: the new merchant class whose power was derived from material wealth. Despite the incredible achievements of the Renaissance and in particular such men as Michelangelo and Leonardo da Vinci whose genius represented a high point of unified, human creativity, the spiritual needs of man were ultimately subjugated by the individual's stronger desire for material security and comfort – an understandable progression in a world which had become divorced from the Whole and the God Within.

Even the Reformation, which was initially influenced by Erasmus's vision of man standing in direct relation to God and which grew out of that rebellious part of the Northern mentality which did not like to be told what and how to worship, betrayed the energy of its origin and became embedded in rigidity. Its foremost champion, Martin Luther, was himself a deeply conservative man who went as far as condemning the peasant revolts of the time because of his obsession with maintaining order. As the Protestant faith became politicized by the German princes rebelling against the authority of Rome, this new movement which had the potential of bringing man closer to the teachings of Christ, came to assume the other extreme of the Germanic character: cold discipline, obedience and dry intellect.

In philosophy, intellect was now completely devoid of spirit with Descartes, the so-called father of modern philosophy, arrogantly insisting that he could prove the existence of God through rational argument. Philosophical enquiry increasingly focused on social and material concerns, science reached new dimensions with Newton's rigid laws pertaining to the physical world, and the spiritual nature of man was firmly pushed back into the hands of conservative

74

orthodoxy. On the other end of the spectrum, the Romantic movement, alienated by this cold, dry mentality, sought to find its own fulfilment through the passion of personal love and an idealization of the 'noble savage' – a genuine quest for a deeper connection between people, but still focusing on outer stimuli rather than the inner connection to a greater Whole.

The great Revolutions in France, America and throughout the Western world consolidated the power of the new, materialistic middle-class, as opposed to liberating the masses – so that, when the Industrial Revolution swept across the great Western powers, there arose a new governing class which used its powers of control in a fundamental way which was different only in nature, not in extent, from the control of the masses which had been exercized for hundreds of years before.

Of course, the Industrial Revolution brought materialism to a height never before experienced and institutionalized new levels of inequality which exist to this day despite so-called democracy. It also created new levels of fear. As man surrounded himself with more and more possessions, the fear of losing this 'wealth' became stronger and stronger. Nationalities became more introverted and fearful of others, leading to the ridiculous merry-go-round of alliances which culminated in the First World War.

Man's creativity had reached its zenith in weapons of mass destruction and his inability to see the innate connection between all men has permitted him to use them. A mere twenty years later, the lessons had not been learnt and the absolute nature of the rational mind's sense of separation was realized in Hitler's destruction of the Jews, only to be repeated in recent years with Saddam Hussein launching chemical weapons against the Kurd minority in his own country.

The reason I felt it necessary to go back into our evolution in this way is to see that the forces of power and control which are pervasive throughout the world must not be judged as either good or evil, but can be seen as a natural progression from man's separation from his original state of Unity. The supremacy of the male over the female and of the rational over the intuitive, the obsession with temporal power and material possessions, the fear and guilt within the psyche of man and the resulting distrust of the individual – all of these have developed as mankind has followed its evolutionary path to become the temporarily dominant species on this planet. If we judge ourselves and our leaders, we are judging our species as a whole.

We cannot of course turn the clock back. What we can do, though, is to use our understanding of the forces which have shaped us in order to bring this duality, this separation back to a more unified sense of the world, where our connection to one another and to the Source of our Being will truly guide our behaviour.

The Modern World

Eric Morse

Just about two hundred years ago, beginning mostly in western Europe, the Earth saw its human progeny enter into the period which we have come to know as the Industrial Revolution. We had been using machinery of sorts for much longer, of course, but now there set in such an intensive development of mechanised manufacturing that we really can date our progressively rapacious exploiting of Earth's resources from the mid to late Eighteenth Century A.D. Immense areas of countryside were depopulated as their peoples were forced into the newly risen cities which swallowed up whole groups of villages and laid them under palls of black smoke poured from factory chimneys; and yet more country scenes, especially picturesque valleys, began to sprout new and ugly hills of black slag as the people there were driven deep underground to bring out massive tonnages of coal for the factories to make their steam power and their smoke. More than one poet of the period, voicing anguish at what was happening, compared the slag-heaps on the skin of Earth to the black pustules on people during outbreaks of the Black Death plague.

But such poets were mere lone voices in the wilderness then, for the comfortable homes and clubs where their works were read were mostly far from the hideous industrial sites themselves; and the steady flow into those homes of cheap and novel products were of great wonder to the buyers, hardly one of whom could be expected to anticipate the devastation to Earth's environment that would set in over the next two centuries as the industrialisation gathered pace. For sure, none suspected that the air might become dangerously close to poisonous over vast areas, that ocean levels might begin to rise and actually menace the bounds of our home-lands, and that the change to the atmosphere's chemistry might expose us to perilous increases of the more damaging constituents of the Sun's radiation. Scarcely anyone outside of the Royal Society even had a clue as to what the chemistry of Earth's air cushion was anyway, and still less any idea of what radiations were present in the taken-for-granted light from the Sun.

Industrialisation did meet with some resistance from those in high places, however, most notably from certain of the landed gentry and from the religious powers in the shape of the Holy Church. Unlike the part which the best of these play today, their resistance then was not for environmental or humanitarian reasons – and certainly not out of concern for wildlife, which churchmen asserted had no souls and which therefore they hunted with as much wanton glee as did any local baron or squire; it was purely a matter of the Churches fearing the rise of a power greater than themselves over the people, and of the ever bolder encroachment upon the Churches' own lands as princelings and governments were encouraged by scientific persuasion and blatant brib-ery to sanction the industrial spread. Capitalism was fast conquering the domains and even the ideological monolithy of catholicism.

Quite rightly, albeit for their own ulterior motives, did the churchmen predict and condemn the rise of a self-blinkering materialist-atheist ideology, especially as it began to spread like a fever among the abject masses of people driven so suddenly into large but very dense estates of housing around the factories and mines where now they laboured. In the main, the new power-class of industrialists held the church at bay by applying the central principle that had given them their power: If you can't beat your opponent in combat, do business with him and beat him there. Some of them sincerely believed that their industrial discoveries and their power derived from them were truly God-given – for sure God had not prevented them – and so they not only continued to attend and benefact the Church as did their rivals in the landed gentry; they also made sure to invite it into the industrial estates and build churches for it there. The Church was already expert at persuading miserable serfs that their barons' power over them was the Will of God for the good of their souls, and that plagues were likewise Divine Will rather than brought on by revolting sanitary conditions that could and should be changed; so now the Church could keep the authority and fear of God alive and well amongst the wage-slaves of industry. No-one could suggest that that was the start of the corruption of religion but it was certainly a new chapter in its grim story.

The blatant hypocrisy of religion justifying the execrable conditions of the industrial scene was of course a major factor in the rise of atheism, especially when it was intelligently expounded by Karl Marx and Friedrich Engels in the *Communist Manifesto*. Their clear concern for the people and their cogent programme for their liberation sounded far closer to the Will of a Loving God than the justification of tyranny spilled out by the Church which, using religion to justify a soulless mammon-worshipping regime, was in reality no less atheist than the two founders of Communism.

Yet religion, even in its worst times and places, has never been without members whose belief is sincere in the extreme, and certainly this was so during the Industrial Revolution. They were to be found, in a minority perhaps, but a vociferous one, within the great-power churches of the Establishment; and they were a vehement majority among the Non-Conformists, Quaker, Methodist, Unitarian and the like, and often with as much will to revolutionary political action as any among the Socialists and Communists.

The response of the authorities to this revolt against oppression was, of course, further oppression; and the response of the oppressed to that, often for the saving of their very lives, was emigration to the Americas. In the wake of emigrants from the previous two centuries, who had fled largely to escape persecution on more directly religious grounds, went new waves seeking wide open spaces again as a release from the prison-like rows of tenements and back-to-back hovels in industrial Europe. And to them was added wave after wave of starving victims of the instability which the Capitalist system was now manifesting – its proneness to successions of economic boom and slump. A final wave came from the remaining agrarian communities on the outskirts of industry, where peasants were being deliberately starved, their crops forcibly destroyed, to drive them to the mills and mines as cheap labour. The infamous potato famine in Ireland, engineered from England, is but one example of what was practised by other powers also elsewhere in Europe.

As it has been so often in the history of great migrations, however, the migrants are far from being the angelic creatures their sympathisers like to imagine. They have been depressed and embittered at home and, for all their courage in venturing on a long uncertain voyage, they are often the weaker brethren of those who stayed at home to fight the tyranny with their skill, their wits and their will to die before they will surrender or run for safety abroad. It should not surprise us, then, that in the free but inevitably harsh environment of wide spaces defended only by a small number of ill equipped native inhabitants, the immigrants 'go wild' like the huns and vandals of old, slaughtering all before them in their own quest for power, territory and wealth. Moving them from within is an urge to have all that their once-hated oppressors in the old home had over them. It was just this that made such barbarians of the Cossacks of the Steppes, and the cowboys and prospectors of the Wild West.

Thus it was that the Industrial Revolution spread to a land which by the end of the Nineteenth Century was already close to being the world's greatest industrial power, and during the first half of our own century grew to surpass the power of all its rivals combined. And while voices of genuine religious faith have never ceased to be heard there, the mammon-orientated philosophy of the U.S.A. has rivalled even the Soviet Union as the apostle of naked atheism and of the utterly narrow self-interests of the power-seekers among humanity. For the American Dream, elevated to the status of a vision by its Hollywood and Broadway enthusiasts, has long been one of success in business to the exclusion of all other considerations; and its record of suppression and even annihilation of all who stood in its way – vegetation, animal, Indian, trade-unionist and rival entrepreneur alike – in the first forty years of this century has seen the Dream take on a reality no less hideous in too many respects than the nightmare that blossomed in the U.S.S.R. Well did Carl Gustav Jung describe the lands of the Red and the White stars as *two lovers who have quarrelled with each other.*

But the United States of America is not essentially any different from any other country in the industrialised world in our time, each of which bears responsibility for the abuse of the technology they have created. That technology is in the main destructive power, even when applied to 'peaceful purposes', and we should note soberly that we are by no means so much its masters as we like to believe. Nuclear power as a source of electrical supply, for example, looks on the face of it to be a wonderful feat of science and engineering which we have chosen to invent just because we are now that clever. Yes, of course, it is a marvel of our science, but also an extremely uneconomic way of producing energy. We have used it for two reasons of circumstance over which we felt we had no choice: To produce the material for the nuclear weapons we might have to use against our feared potential enemies, and to sustain our electricity supply if Earth's fast-diminishing reserves of oil should dry up on us – or if its increasing scarcity should tempt the countries which produce it to demand full market value for it.

That, of course, is what the whole present Gulf Crisis is all about when all the hypocrisy is cast aside. It is all but nauseating to hear the pious public show of wailing for hapless Kuwait coming from a power which vowed publicly ten years ago that it would use its military might there if it should ever feel its own oil needs from that region to be at risk, and coming from another power which itself ruled Kuwait as a colony until it became militarily untenable at a reasonable cost, and a business deal with its native rulers looked a cheaper prospect!

The fact we must now face is that the Gulf Crisis is but one, the first if you like to call it so, of a hurricane-force storm of crises that are about to burst upon us because we have all but torn our planet apart with two hundred years of rapacious plunder of its resources, minerals, coal, oil, uranium, soil, herbage, animal and marine life, oxygen and ozone, until it can give little more without becoming mortally wounded and no longer able to function as our home. We also are part of its animal life, and though our cleverness just may preserve us long enough to be its last remaining species – and there is no guarantee of that – the fate of extinction awaits us as surely as it has already come to so many other species in this century. The few who warned us three decades ago were easily dismissed as Jeremiahs or drug-soaked hippies but today governments are holding more and more frantic conferences about the situation as its grim truth sinks in even upon them to threaten the very stability of the power they hold.

They would have done well thirty years ago to remember that, unpopular as Jeremiah is (and was in his own days too), his sorrowful predictions came true! And perhaps the hippies also, their inbuilt inertia quietened by their drugs, were free to see the future with a clarity that the rest of us did not want to see, still held as we were by an inertia which wanted no change that we ourselves did not choose of our own volition. There is no time now to pussyfoot with proposals for what we shall do about the environment in the next century, nor even at the tip end of this one: That will be too late. If we must be in error with our timing – and we cannot help that – then we shall do better to say that we have months in which to put matters right, not years. Perhaps we have fifty months, not just ten – I have no magic clock – but we certainly do not have fifty years, not even ten.

It is one thing, however, to stress how urgently we must do something, quite another to say just how we must act. If those who rule us have been reluctant to tell us just how imminent or perilous our situation is, that is not only because they are not themselves clear or all of one mind as to what should be done; it is also because they know only too well that people facing a crisis act all too often out of panic, fear and short-sighted urges for self-preservation which inevitably bring about precisely the destruction that is most feared. And this is especially so when the leaders are, as just said, by no means agreed as to what leadership they should give. Leaders are, by common consensus, supposed to know what to do. When they don't, and cannot hide their disability, then they risk that same popular consensus turning its frustration and fear negatively upon them instead of intelligently towards the real causes of the crisis, and the result is a wholesale breakdown of order in which nothing useful at all can be done.

What I wish to offer in my own final chapter is what I see as the principles that should underpin our course of action – principles which take account of all that we know about ourselves, our origins locked away in our subconscious memories, our present state of consciousness, and what we may expect our state to become in the near future. Upon this knowledge and with what we now know of our inertia and how to deal with it, and with what we now know of the condition of our world today, we really can act in such ways that our path into the new conditions before us may be trodden with the minimum of pain, stress and damage to ourselves, our fellow beings of all life's species, and our planet.

Crisis indeed we are facing, but we contain within us all that we need in order to surmount every danger and challenge, and we can look forward to a wonderful future if we just get our approach to it on the right footing now.

Mind Freed From Its Fetters

Eric Morse

It is proposed in this book to present . . . certain speculations about the trend of present forces, speculations which, taken all together, will build up an imperfect and very hypothetical, but sincerely intended forecast of the way things will probably go in this new century. H. G. Wells: *Anticipations* (publ: 1902).

Mr Wells, writing in 1902, was about to launch into a broad discussion of just about everything which he reasoned was likely to happen in the Twentieth Century. And, in that now relatively unknown volume of his many formidable works, he predicted what was to come with remarkable – many would say uncanny – accuracy. Diehard atheist and scientific materialist, Wells was almost alone in failing to recognise just how psychic and prophetically clairvoyant he was, clinging grimly to the assertion that all his visionary capacity was due to his calculating brain alone, never to any reception of advice from any other plane of Being – in which he had no belief.

Wells was a very unhappy man, for, while clearly fore-seeing catastrophe pile upon disaster as the years would pass, his atheism would not allow him to receive also any assurance that there really was some unseen guiding watch over it all, and that there could ever be any worthwhile outcome to this troubled century, through the first half of which he lived. So it was that his last published work, in the final year of his life,

1946, was an epilogue to his *Short History of the World*, a final chapter which he headed: *Mind at the End of its Tether*. It is in tribute to him that I have adapted his title in the heading for my chapter here. I am even hopeful that he, of course now knowing of those higher planes of life into which he himself has entered, may actually be among my inspirers in what I now write.

We are poised now on the very brink of changes going far beyond what was revealed to Wells, changes involving whole other dimensions of Space and Time, only the skimpiest and most imperfect hints of which did he receive and pass on to us in *The Time Machine*. Wells wrote in 1946 that Mind was at the end of its tether, meaning that, of course, in the despairing way we say it when we feel we just cannot take any further stress.

Since his passing we have been veritably rushing to snap that tether, or fetter, as I have restyled it, and already many thousands of us are a very different creature from Man as Wells and his contemporaries knew the species. The ranks of atheism, materialism as a philosophy, have dwindled at a staggering pace since the early 1960s, the demise of the Communist world being as much due to the newly rising awareness of the spiritual dimensions of life as to any of its tensions from tyranny, corruption, mismanagement and interference from the West – all of which have of course played their parts as well.

Conventional religions, notably Muslim and Christian, in that order of success, are enjoying an influx to their flocks as a result, for people sensing within themselves some voice stirring them, often to their discomfort, and demanding that they listen, naturally turn to the mosques and churches where they hope to find some confirmation that the inner promptings are genuine and healthy.

But while some do find comfort there, at least as many feel their inner voices urging them to look beyond the established authorities on spiritual guidance, urging them to ask and discuss with others all manner of questions about religion, astrology, psychic faculties, witchcraft, UFOs, possible superior beings watching over us – topics which twenty years earlier they would have been sure were signs that they needed psychiatric treatment. The scale of this new awareness, and with it the feeling that the old authorities do not have adequate answers, is seen in the success in recent years of such regular events as the 'Festival of Mind, Body & Spirit', and the 'Psychics & Mystics Fair' – events which would not have been tolerated only a few decades earlier, even in freedom-loving Britain and America, and would not have drawn enough visitors to cover the expenses even if they had been held.

What is happening to these people is the rising, like sap in the early Spring, of a force within them that is far more than just psychology's 'unconscious' rising to haunt them from the past – this unconscious **is** intruding, true enough, and on an unprecedented scale, but only because the whole Mind of Man is breaking out of its habitual barriers.

Our familiar view of the world has been a world of three dimensions only, with events and people appearing and then departing according to the tick of a clock called Time, whatever that may be. But today, for thousands of very baffled people, that clock seems sometimes to do the very oddest things.

Memories flood in from the past, not just 'as if it were only yesterday' but with such force that 'it is all happening right now!' Happening again? 'Well, maybe it did happen once before – it seems that familiar – yet there is some kind of life-force in it now that you don't get with mere memories, do you?' And then again, 'It's not like a dream in the ordinary sense, all jumbled and silly. These people talk to me about quite sensible things, and as though they half-know me and I feel I ought to know them but can't quite place them. Sometimes they know my past even better than I can remember it myself; other times they drop strong hints about my future, and turn out to be right; still other times they don't seem to be quite human, and they examine me carefully like doctors or zoologists finding out exactly how I work.' Who are they? Where are they from? 'They don't say; they might if I asked, I suppose, but I don't quite like to; they don't encourage questions.'

What I have just described is typical of an interview with any of a score or more of people who have come to just me alone, only one of dozens or hundreds who try to help people understand what is happening to them. And the people who come have not been on hashish or vodka or been branded as psychotics; they go on working normally for most of their time, and, in the main, they only receive those strange experiences when quietly alone on free days, or during their sleep, when they have been quite accustomed to 'ordinary' dreams, or to not noticing that they dream at all. Their experiences vary so widely that I have been able only to present a tiny pot-pourri with the main features of most of them.

Of course, experiences like this are recorded right back into ancient history: Moses, Ezekiel, the Virgin Mary, the Prophet Muhammad and saints as recent as Bernadette of Lourdes all come to mind. So does the philosopher of our own century, J. W. Dunne, whose angelic visitor guided him to produce his remarkable theory of Time as a further dimension of Space, or rather as just one of an infinity of dimensions of Space. His major treatise, *An Experiment with Time*, is in our bibliography, as also is his final work, *Intrusions?* in which he at last broke his silence about his angelic visitations, having feared earlier that to have spoken of them would have cast doubt among his fellows as to the validity of his scientific qualifications.

The first really vivid signs that something new was happening to us came in the late 1940s and on through the 50s in the form of a remarkably large number of 'UFO' sightings and 'Close Encounters of a Third Kind'. The same has continued ever since with alternating spells of high activity and quiet spells, and it is highly significant that it has been happening to people leading active business lives, far removed from either spare time or inclination to dwell upon things spiritual or religious. When someone is profoundly and demonstrably affected by what they have seen, felt or heard, then that experience is real even though a thousand doctors refuse to say it is. Were it not so, it would leave no effects. The same doctors, we may add, would undoubtedly have denied the reality of the experiences of Isaiah, Jesus and Muhammad, to mention but a sample, – indeed the doctors and lawyers in their own times **did** deny it, even killed some of them for their revelations, yet the reality of their experiences is with us still to this day.

As to just what the reality of the UFO experiences is, we must not as yet be drawn into too much debate about that either. Dr Carl Jung, as formidable a thinker as has yet investigated the matter, came down mainly in favour of regarding UFOs as an *inner* experience, yet without discounting that those same inner entities might equally have some *external* – even extra terrestrial – source.

My own studies of UFO and kindred experiences suggest strongly that they are visitations upon us both from higher realms of existence of which we are just becoming faintly aware, and also from long past periods in our history which at our 'normal' level of awareness we have forgotten, yet in the depths of our subconsciousness we almost do remember, which is why the visitors seem almost but not quite known to us. There is also the matter of our nervous reluctance to ask them for information, as though they might then tell us something we decidedly don't want to remember – not just something personal to us, from which we might just suffer mild neurotic 'karmic' hangovers, but a memory, or memories, deeply affecting our whole identity as the human race.

Within that buried memory that we don't quite like to ask about is the matter of the gigantic catastrophe some twelve thousand years ago when our Sun's binary companion exploded, causing a major rearrangement of our planetary system, and so nearly wiping out life on Earth that what survived was so mutated as to constitute a whole new set of species here, humanity included. Whatever 'we' were before then has perished, and what we are now has replaced it. The story, told in obscure hints in our ancient holy books and our mythology, is a sobering reminder that Earth and Heaven alike are in a continuous process of Evolution; and that while its Life and Soul forces are eternal, the forms they assume in flesh and blood are distinctly temporary, albeit each with a life-run of several thousand years.

The human animal life-form as we know it today, then, cannot be expected to go on forever, or certainly not as the dominant life-form of this planet. Other species have ruled before us and we have displaced them, though some may still be around us as mere relics of what once they were – the remarkable communal organisation of ants, bees, ocean-ic mammals and the like have often been seen as evidence of their erstwhile dominance, and some descriptions of the 'UFO' visitors have borne a close resemblance to some of such species. If that is so, then clearly our own subliminal, immortal selves must recognise having once had those other forms, and may well be trying to prepare us for yet another change to come.

In that case, why, it may be asked, are we generally so struck with fear in these experiences? If the real, immortal self knows it has done all this before, and has evidently come through all the better for it, why our panic? Just ask anyone who, through drugs, hypnotism or any esoteric training has experienced an 'altered state of consciousness'. Most will tell you that, in the critical moment of change, they felt panic that they were about to cease to exist. Only afterwards did they discover that some 'core Self' within them remained unaffected and never lost its ongoing sense of identity. What is at work causing the fear is again the *inertia* of our existing physical nervous structure, resisting the drive that now threatens to transform that structure and adapt us for new life-conditions in which more of our creative capacities, at present only latent potentials, will come into full usage. We are again like the child just attaining puberty, wary and even afraid of an evolution it does not yet understand, and with the process of reaching understanding made all the more difficult because of that poor linkage between cerebellum and cortex – that present inbuilt state of 'sin'.

I have spent quite some print, now, on one of the most extreme areas of our expanding awareness, one which still has very many people doubting its validity, notwithstanding that the general awareness of survival after death and of other realms of existence has grown in such measure that the idea of at least some measure of communication being possible with these realms is now more widely accepted. One is no longer a freak for being a Spiritualist, even though critics, myself included, stop short of calling that an adequate basis for a religion. Spiritualism, it now seems to me, has spent a hundred years preparing us for something even more important than getting to know that we survive after death and still retain our sense of identity even after that huge change of state.

It has been leading us on to discover not just departed friends a few steps beyond death's frontier (life's frontier), but a breathtaking discovery of our own immortal immensity way, way beyond those first few steps. More and more people are undergoing such deep voyages of self-discovery: bizarre to begin with, confusing and frightening too, yet with no longer any doubt that they are the opening of a doorway within us leading to an unprecedented wholeness of our Being, a wholeness that takes us ever nearer to a sense of true and sure kinship with the boundless Source of All Being, and, with that kinship, a sense of safety and security such as we have not known, at least since we evolved two almost disconnected brain systems.

As that security grows in us, so those disconnections are under repair – or we should say better that connections are now being built in that have never been installed before. Our journey through the state of 'sin', with all its feel of weakness and fear, is all but completed. Earth too will be safe because we shall know that we are safe, safe upon it, safe from each other and from all else that dwells here, safe because no part of us is any longer disconnected from any other part, all the way to the Source. On the road towards this new state, we have learned by sheer intellect whole volumes of knowledge that only the evolution of our cortex, seat of intellect, has made possible. That is why we had to make the journey that way, creating for ourselves the prize that has made the rough passage worthwhile. Christ, the Messiah, the Mahdi, whatever we variously call it, is about to make its Second Coming, and in brilliant Glory – not as one single person but as that Quality secure in all of Us.

3

Spirituality in Action

Surrender and Sacrifice

Denise Cooney

I have recently been talking on the telephone with one of my clients and it has occurred to me that people are losing track of their path. While I am listening to the person speaking, I am also hearing a very disturbing message that many people have been delivering lately. There seems to be a lack of understanding of what surrender is truly all about.

For the truth is that surrender does not mean always seeing the other person's side of things and then allowing yourself to become a doormat because a) you have been studying metaphysics and can see their lesson; b) you have the patience to wait until they see your side of things, and c) you are waiting to see if they will awaken so you will handle the pain because that is surrender, understanding, and letting go.

So many so-called 'New Age' teachers say that all you have to do is to not empower a situation and it will either go away or it will do as you have visualized. Wrong! This is where I see people stuck and not moving forward. They call, telling me they have prayed for so and so to 'see the Light', or they have tried to change their work place, or they tell people that they must work with more positive attitudes because their negativity is bringing them down. The immaturity, ignorance and arrogance that is being taught to people is causing many people to wonder if they have lost their faith because everything in their lives isn't so beautiful. The one phrase that I have been hearing every day and with more frequency from people is: 'If only they could see what they are doing to . . . their children . . . themselves . . . others . . . the environment . . . etc!'

So, what do I mean by ignorance, arrogance or immaturity? It is to take Ancient Truths, which need a lifetime or two to perfect, and to sell them as a weekend extravaganza in the hope of making a quick buck. It is those Teachers who have forgotten that the work they do along the Path is not for self-aggrandizement; nor is the study of Truth without its moments of doubt.

The reason the Mystery Schools are called a Mystery is because these teachings take dedication. It is truly made of hard work and does call for us to **sacrifice** our ego and allow God or Spirit to work through us. Therefore, it is *not up to you* to try to change, visualize or try to convince any one person or thing that your way is their way.

Think about it! Isn't that what the missionaries did to ancient tribes that had very sacred beliefs unto themselves? You cannot feel that you have lost your power or faith because your wife, husband, lover, mother, father, brother, sister, employer or employee or whoever hasn't changed, even though you put it out there to the universe for them to do so. That is what I mean by arrogance. Who are you to think that you have gotten it more together than anyone else? What did Christ once say? 'Why see the splinter in your brother's eye when there is a plank in your own?' How about putting your belief system to work?

What I am trying to say is it is not up to you or me to force someone to be realized. That shows our level of lack of understanding when we deliberately try to change a situation. No one is off their Path. The twists and turns an individual chooses are self-inflicted. If we go out of our way to change the course of their mighty river, it's like trying to bend steel in your bare hands. I don't know about you, but I am not Superman!

We sometimes think we actually know better than God

when we try to force change. What is hard to reconcile within ourselves is that the only person we can change is ourselves and even that is sometimes seemingly impossible. So, how could we, with our rudimentary consciousness, see the overall plan?

Maybe . . . just maybe . . . that person you are trying to change so intensely because you 'love' them so much is really silently teaching you a lesson.

The Law of Acceptance is not passively letting someone walk all over you, but learning, from the innermost aspect of yourself, to let the situation quietly be. Acceptance is very hard. If you believe in the power of prayer, affirmation, meditation or whatever gets you motivated to seek your higher pathway, just focus in on what lesson you are to learn today, how you can work on yourselves to release the control and to shift the focus away from your desired outcome and work from there.

Here is an example. Suppose you have decided to become a television producer. You are not sure how to go about it but you start by visualizing what you want to happen once you are a producer. Then you go about studying and preparing in classes and actually land a job in your desired field. But, much to your surprise, you are not working as a producer or even as an assistant. You find yourself in the position of a gofer, who has to run around after this and that. This is not exactly as you had pictured it but, what the heck, you persevere and find that, after years of attempting to go for gold, you haven't either made the contacts or the promotions to put you in your original intentioned field.

So many things could happen at this point. You could try again and approach it from a different angle. Or you may find that you are no longer interested for many different reasons. If you think you have failed at your original goal, then you may find yourself spending countless days, months or years reminiscing about what could have been.

This is likened to one who has lost their faith or someone who may feel the Universe didn't give them their desired good. Who are we really to always think that we can always know what the future should be like? We always mould our future and destiny, but part of the path is also to be open to rich and wonderful surprises. When we accept our destiny or what fate has put before us, and when we see or try to see that it wasn't in our highest and best interest – when we do all this, however difficult this is to do, and when we move on, then will we find that something greater was waiting for us.

Back to the person who never made it in the world of television. Suppose that person allowed Faith to truly guide them. They might find that the small ego was guiding them all along and that the higher field had nothing to do with entertainment but rather with something more beneficial, for that soul to grow in another arena of life. (That is not to infer for one moment that entertainment can not provide lessons. Certainly from the standpoint of letting go of the ego it is probably one of the hardest places to learn humility!)

Sacrifice is underrated as a portion of the Pathwork, especially by the 'New Age' set, who see it as something negative. Why would one have to sacrifice anything if one is *in the light*?

I guess Christ, Krishna, Buddha and all those old-fangled Masters had it all wrong! Why would Christ ask for such a negative experience as to be crucified, or carry the cross, or have a crown of thorns? Sure, Christ taught high mystical Truth. So did Buddha, and what was wrong with him was that he was in a poverty state of consciousness. How dare he sit under the Banyon tree and ask people to ask for nothing?! How about those native Americans and their corny belief that everything is sacred and we cannot own the land? Well, golly, if these people had taken prosperity workshops, imagine how much more powerful they would have been! Imagine Christ making his teachings available to the masses for **free**. Unthinkable. How about him stilling the water and walking on it? If he was really powerful, we would have heard him channel some being that came before him!

What I am trying to get across with all of this is that, since the beginning of time, our time that is, humans have been put on the planet to grow. To deny our feelings and pretend that only the perfect live in perfection is to deny that we are human. Christ had his off days, too!

Self-Development

Eric Morse

We are probably all familiar from our school days with the aches and pains that ensued after our first lessons in the gym and on the sports field. (Whether these were truly voluntary or not is beside the point, we did them to ourselves.) Those aches were of course the result of purely mechanical inertia – muscles having to do what they hadn't done before.

But there is another area of inertial distress for many pupils at school: the very fact of having to impose upon themselves, at someone else's orders, disciplined time-keeping, paying of close attention to subjects that are actually boring them, and then proving that they have absorbed those lessons by coming out well in exams – all this imposes inertial stresses not only on the calculating mechanisms of the brain but also upon the emotional system at precisely the time when it is most strongly urging a resolute, even a rebellious show of independence and self-determination. There is something like a three-way pull upon us at that time: along a centreline we may write 'carry on as the child you were' but pulling away sharply to the right is a new force saying 'you're in the army now, so take your orders from the man up there at the blackboard', while pulling with just as much force to the left is a force urging 'you're your own man now, so tell 'em all to go play their own game of soldiers'.

The force to the right can usually count, in the end, on getting support from the parents who are the dominant feature on that centreline; and so we fit into the system; but if that 'difficult age' is not handled with great skill by those directing our course through it, our further evolution and development may become very stressed and distorted indeed. A vital part of what we should be learning at that time is the fine art of compromise, the art which includes recognising what we judge to be our own true needs and interests, yet including the possibility that if we endure with good humour what someone else thinks we ought to be taught, then we may eventually find that this has also some use to which we can put it.

That is how the matter will go if both ourselves and the parents and teachers involved adopt that attitude about it. But if any party among the three, especially the parents and/or teachers, apply only the force of command without humour and reasonableness, then the result is something like the example we used of getting that garden roller moving when it lay at rest in a rut. Those newly aroused centres in ourselves are something of a well-oiled and brand new roller in that rut. Yes, there is a high resistance to start with but then, once set in motion, those centres charge headlong with all the inertial power of their teenage energy in them.

The result is all too often a whole aviary of burning resentments and neurotic, maybe even psychotic, distortions of the life pattern as each causative event during those critical years becomes an entity and a power centre in its own right and with its own inertia. In the extreme, which is unhappily by no means uncommon, these resentful entities go all the way to becoming what psychology terms 'fragmented personalities', presenting themselves like turns in a variety show as their owner swings from mood to mood, to mood. The same elders who called them up like a bungling sorcerer's apprentice evoking sprites from the deeps are now saddled with the task of banishing them again or bringing them into some degree of peace and harmony with the world in which the damaged pupil is going to have to live. Only in this real version of the old story, no master sorcerer appears at the end of the tale to restore peace with a magic word!

We must be just as careful in any programme of entirely voluntary self-development we undertake that we do not perpetrate just that same kind of violence upon ourselves. It may come as a surprise, and even be disbelieved that we actually can do that – but we can and we all too often do. And as we are moving on through times of change more rapid and far-reaching than we have known for many whole centuries, or even many millennia, we shall find we are committing all manner of spiritual, psychological, emotional and physical mayhem upon ourselves unless we learn quite deliberately how to go the right way about coping with that change. I make no exalted claims to having all the answers here, and may myself fall prey to my own mistakes just like anyone else, but my own experiences in the course of life, and what I have observed from the experiences of colleagues and clients, may give me the right to round off this chapter with a few little snippets that should be helpful to others.

Many people who undertake some chosen programme of personal or individual Development are much alarmed when they begin to manifest symptoms they have not expected, physically, emotionally, mentally, ethically and in some other ways too. And if they themselves are not thus troubled, then certainly many of the people around them and watching them may be worried by what they observe of the one developing. Just a few examples from my own observations will explain what I mean.

'Jim' (not his/her real name, of course) took up quite early in life with the self-development principles taught by the famous esoteric teacher G. I. Gurdjieff, a half-psychologist, half-mystic whose principal theme was that we are all like sheep in a field whose owner, having no fence to put round his land, hypnotised us all to believe that there is a fence around us. Gurdjieff's scheme of self training is aimed at removing that delusion and thus freeing us from all the bagwash that our past conditioning has heaped upon us. So far, so good, and it is largely what, throughout this present chapter, we have been saying must happen. Jim, however, failed to distinguish within that bagwash between

what could (A) be totally discarded as no longer valid, and
(B) what is still valid, notwithstanding its origins in the
distant past, and (C) what may indeed be no longer valid
for one who has seen through its weaknesses, but must still
be respected if we are to live in peace, goodwill and safety
among the mass of people who have not yet seen through
it, and for whom it is thus **still** valid. One unhappy result
of Jim's failure here is that he has his own rules by which
he decides when to steal things and when not to, and leads
in consequence a risky life in which both his liberty and the
considerable esteem in which others hold him may be taken
away at any moment.

The lesson – no need to call it the moral – from that story
is simply in the matter of those three distinctions, especially
(C) which is the one on which Jim has really come unstuck.
Of course it would be ideal to have a society in which we can
simply take home what we need and, as Jim certainly does,
give of our services to society as best we are able in return
for what we take. But that is not the way society is now, and
just flouting its rules will not make it go that way. What Jim
has actually done is to have stripped the cover off his teenage
resentment of the rules then imposed on him, and tried to
banish them with the same violence that was used to impose
them. He may well have banished the rules to some extent,
but the violence remains with its inertia as powerful as ever;
and now it must seek some other substance upon which to
fasten its energy, that substance being the goods in various
shops.

A second example is the married couple 'Harry' and 'Jill',
both born into one of the most rigid of the old religions, but
who have long since written that off as something that should
have sunk with the ark, and have followed up another line
of esoteric development with a master-figure who teaches
what is alleged to be the 'ancient wisdom' from which the
aforesaid religion is but a corruption and a degeneration.
Again, so far, so good, and much of that master's teaching
is probably pretty near to the truth.

But Harry and Jill have not found the peace and liberty

they expected from this courageous break with their past conditioning. On the contrary, he finds himself bound with intolerable rigidity to the demands of his professional job, while she wavers between finding no orgasmic satisfaction for herself from their sexual relationship, and feeling guiltily that she is failing to give him any in return. In both cases they suffer an almost continuous barrage of physical complaints, not exactly dangerous but certainly distressing enough to interfere seriously with the smooth run of life for them. Eye, ear and headache troubles are especially noticeable, matters which both are reading as symbolic of some deeper problem that is less clear to them.

Their case is perhaps the most characteristic of the kind of distress met with during voluntary development, and their reading of the underlying problem quite correct. What we have inherited through conception, or from previous life experience, is as much a part of us as, say, our coccis or our appendix – both remnants of our evolution from a creature with two stomachs and a tail, both parts for which we have no further use but which we cannot remove without great damage to us, no matter how clearly we recognise their obsoleteness. We have to carry them along with us as passengers, so to speak, and no harm is done so long as we do not resent their continued presence nor try to digest with the remnant stomach, nor wag the tail.

And so it is with our cultural, religious, mental and emotional inheritance. It is part of us forever, and we must accept that. What affects our health, happiness and further growth is how we accept it. Resent it, condemn it for the damage it has done in the past, and we resent and condemn a part of ourselves – with every danger that the disease of resentment will spread through us until we are resenting so much of ourselves that there is scarcely a pain-free part left in us. Resent it with guilt for having ever believed and practised such stuff, and we are imposing that condition commonly called Karma, an obligation seemingly from God to pay up for everything we ever did in our days of ignorance. It is the condition which my late wife and wise teacher called a *celestial neurosis* and of no less harm to us than any other neurosis.

But, suppose we accept even the worst of that inheritance with the same good humour that most of us would feel towards, say, having once believed in Father Christmas, or that the Moon is made of cheese. Dealing with the inertia of our past selves is really no more difficult than that. I know that I inherited one hell of a load of misery from my mother, bereaved at age eleven, and from the wretched state of the sexual relationship between her and my father, and so on; I am told and I believe that I led several previous lives as very nasty kinds of power-hungry ecclesiast and alchemist, along with having 'baby-snatched' a young wife from her ailing mother, callously deserting the same wife in a later incarnation for the glory of command in a rebel army – a long, long tale with little to be proud of in it.

What is all that now? Cause for ongoing guilt which will only drive me into further confused abuse of myself and others? Or rich experience from which I have learned much, and which I can now use to understand others, and as material for the stories I love to write? In the earlier years of this life I did indeed suffer guilt, confusion and sickness from those buried records, and if there ever was any paying to be done for it all, I surely did it then. But any further paying ceased from the day I realised that, as Omar Khayyam said:

> *The moving finger writes and, having writ,*
> *Moves on, nor all thy piety nor wit*
> *Shall lure it back to cancel half a line,*
> *Nor all thy tears wash out one word of it.*

Perhaps we have developed most healthily and most effectively when we have learned that all that past battling in ignorance and folly was being watched all the time by the Soul and the God within us, whatever and however we may call that inner self of which we still know so little. It was being watched patiently by a wisdom which knew all the time where it was leading, and was always satisfied that we should arrive there exactly on time. Our blunders and pains along the way are caused **only** by our dogged refusal to hand over our experiences to that God Within, which alone has the wisdom and power, to put them into their right context within our long story, to take from them their inertia of pain and guilt, to make of them the rich source material upon which we can build lives healthier and happier than we have ever dreamt possible.

'Confess' our 'sins' in our habitual manner of guilt and expectation of retribution for them, instead of this joyous delivery of them into safe All-Wise hands, and we are only clinging onto them still, clinging to them with our tiny canful of understanding that makes us about as safe with them as a monkey with a nuclear bomb. No guru, no elaborate system of esoteric teachings and exercises can do anything more for us when we have reached that understanding; for then we have truly entered into the 'Aquarian Age', the age of humans each finding that self-understanding and true self-assurance by which we feel no threat from another, and therefore make no threat upon another but dwell in truly secure Peace.

Spiritual Living on the Physical Plane I

Nick Bamforth

When I wrote about the return of the Christ Consciousness, I was referring to a consciousness which would take root within many people, not just in one individual – and this is the key to the changes which are going to take place in our world in these next few decades and beyond. We cannot look to our 'leaders' to change the way in which we perceive reality: they are merely at the apex of the pyramid and are concerned with the material world which appears to them to be the only reality.

We all know, deep down within us, that we as individuals are the ones who are going to create change. This is not being élitist, as there are thousands of people throughout the world who are beginning to come into a greater awareness of their own consciousness and strength. All of us have much to do to learn and grow within ourselves before we can assume our mantle of power, which is why this chapter is all about what we can do within ourselves, rather than about things we can do to change others.

What I must stress is that whatever happens in the Middle East or in any other area of conflict or disaster is **nothing to do with you**, unless you are in the midst of it. This is going to be a time when the old energies of power and control are going to play themselves out, often against each other. There may well be horrendous things happening, which will be presented in graphic detail on our television screens, but, if you put any energy but love and compassion into such situations, you will be feeding the flames of the forces which are in conflict.

There will be more great famines in Africa and throughout the world, and we shall also be witness to this. But, remember the famine in Ethiopia which moved so many people in recent years and think of the dignity of the millions of souls who suffered this hardship. We in the so-called 'civilized' world put ourselves up on a pedestal above the more 'primitive' cultures; little did we realize that, by their calm acceptance of their lot, these starving people helped to raise the consciousness of those of us who were watching their deprivation from the comfort of our homes.

This is not the time to see ourselves in any way superior, or for that matter inferior, to another, as all living creatures are equal in 'God's eyes'. As we walk through our lives, we meet so many people of different races, behaviour and mentality, but each of us is going through our own growth at our own pace. We may become impatient with or intolerant of others, but, in doing so, we are immediately falling into the abyss of separation and of judgment. We must, as Christ said, take the plank out of our own eye before we try to take the speck out of another's.

There will be many people standing up on their pedestal telling us that this is the right way or that is the wrong way. Indeed, one can easily recognize the many 'false teachers' which Christ talked about by seeing how they insist that their's is the only way. They fall into the trap of seeing the world in terms of absolute precepts which apply to everyone; they arrogantly choose to impose an 'objective' reality, as if they are the only ones in touch with some higher truth. Beware of those who use the word 'objective' when putting forward their view; in this fleeting world of change, the only reality is our own experience, and therefore any truth must be subjective, something felt by one's individual conscience.

I have no doubt that many of you reading this book will have gone through a pretty intense time in your lives recently, and this is all to do with the preparation for the times to come. Everyone with whom I have worked over the past couple of years has been through an intensity of experience which has made them re-examine and often let go of many old habits of behaviour which only served to hold them back from moving forwards towards the new, heightened awareness breaking through into their consciousness.

These habits had a great deal to do with the old perception of self which many people hold on to. In our continuous need to strive forwards, we have in the past set specific goals for ourselves and tended to perceive ourselves in certain rigid ways which quite often had more to do with the way others perceived us than the way we truly were. Periods of pain and introspection often sweep these false perceptions away, but losing the familiarity of them frequently leaves a gap which is yearning to be filled.

This is one of the greatest tests for anyone who has chosen the spiritual path. Not to know where we are going can evoke great fear, and this is the point at which our faith is truly put to the test. Do we force ourselves into some new position for security's sake, or do we trust that our path will become clear at the right time?

I would like to say at this point that I do not know a single person who really knows where they are going at this particular stage in time. This is for a very good reason. The world is going to change to such a fundamental degree in the next few years that knowing where you are going would be an illusion, whereby you would lock yourself into a pattern which would prevent you from being swept along in the wake of any wind of change which may come along. Many of us will find ourselves doing things in a few years which we could never imagine at this point in time.

That is why all we can do is to live in the present and let the future take care of itself – something which few of us have had much experience in doing. The essence of living in the present is stilling the mind, so that one does not always need to put energy into concerns about a future which is, anyway, so unsure. I have never in the past been

one to push other people into meditation, but the bombard-
ment of outside energies is increasing so much that it is now
very important to put a certain period of time to one side
regularly each day so that you can go into the stillness of
your inner self and open yourself up to the guidance that
is there for you. I am not going to tell you how long or
how to meditate, as this is a personal thing. I personally go
outside for five minutes first thing every morning. You may
prefer to sit or lie listening to music or whatever – it does not
matter, as long as you find this place within you on a regular
basis, for it is only when you begin to find your quiet space
within that the still, small voice makes itself heard.

If you look back over your life, you will see that there
are a very small number of **major** decisions which you
have made and which have really altered your life. In our
day-to-day existence, our rational minds dwell on so many
little problems to be dealt with that we often lose any sense
of the 'Big Picture'. In my experience, certainly all the important, major decisions I have made have just come out of the
blue, but have impinged upon my consciousness so strongly
that I have not been able to run away from them. It is likely
that such 'thoughts from nowhere' will be coming to all of
us more and more: if they do so, follow what feels right
and learn to distinguish between this voice of intuition and
the voice of fear which always thinks up excuses why you
should not make a leap into the unknown.

Faith is the knowledge that there is a part of you, not
subject to your rational understanding, which sees the Big
Picture and leads you to your highest Good. It has nothing
to do with the traditional, religious faith in an external God,
but is that part of you which sees the connection between all
things and understands that your intuition is your personal
connection to the Whole.

This is where the power of the individual comes in. This
is no longer the time to do the things which you feel you
ought to do or which other people want you to do. It is the
time to follow your own conscience, which is tied in to the
consciousness of Love. Within this consciousness, the very

act of following your own inner Truth, your own growth and the raising of your vibration is intricately tied in to the growth and raising of vibration of the planet as a whole. By trusting yourself rather than judging yourself, by loving others rather than judging them, you create an energy around you that not only attracts the highest and best into your own life, but will also affect others around you without you even having to utter a single word.

So what is Love? First of all, it is not an emotion; it is a state of being. We are so bombarded by 'love songs' and 'love stories' that we fail to see that 'romantic love' has more to do with our own needs and expectations than with Love itself. In searching for our perfect partner, we are indeed searching for Unity, unity with another being as an expression on the physical plane of a deeper union with the Whole or God. Yet, for so many of us, the idea of a personal love is wrapped up with much that is emotionally unresolved within us and we often seek in others what we are looking for in ourselves.

Love on a Universal level has no such ties. Love is seeing people as they are, without judgment, and feeling the connection with them. Even more than that, it is seeing the Divine in every single, living being. It is the bond which unites us all in the human condition. Love is expansive. It is the active projection of ourselves into the lives of others – not in the respect of entering into people's lives and interfering with their destiny, but of lifting humanity out of the illusion of separation and into Unity within itself.

The opposite of love is judgment, both of self and others. Judgment is the essence of separation. It is that part of us which sees something we do not like within ourselves and cuts ourselves off from it. Judgment and guilt go hand in hand. If you do something about which you feel remorse, you have two choices: either you feel the sadness and understand that this is something you never wish to do again, or you beat yourself over the head, see yourself as a bad and unworthy person and usually end up doing exactly the same again. This is the source of addiction: the more you judge a part of yourself and separate yourself from your action, rather than taking responsibility for it and learning from it, the more you give it an independent energy of its own, ensuring that it will return to you with renewed force.

This is what the dark side is all about. On the global and political level, we can see this as an energy which has created a force all of its own, seemingly beyond the control of man. It is separation brought to its furthest point, where man judges man, where good and evil are seen as absolute truths, where two self-righteous forces seek to destroy each other as one sees the dark within the other without seeing it within itself.

But, just as important, this is an energy which exists within every shade of existence. We are all seemingly being confronted with those aspects of ourselves which we judge and even fear – and this is where the great challenge lies. As we go through our lives, those aspects of our being which have been hidden so long within our subconscious are suddenly beginning to rise up without warning, so that we are being forced to examine what we truly believe in and how we perceive ourselves and others.

To say to you that all we can do is to go through what we have to go through may seem both gloomy and rather unhelpful, but it is quite simply an understanding that the difficult changes and learning being experienced by people at this time are part of a process whereby we are being prepared to move from one level of vibration to another. We must work through the unresolved emotional aspects of our lives, integrating them into our being rather than separating ourselves from them through judgment. None of us as individuals can attain a true sense of peace and balance within ourselves until we have done this and are fully aware of our own divine nature, rather than continuously doubting our self-worth.

Our rational mind has been a major factor in our evolution as a species, but it is also that part of us which always must see ourselves in comparison with other people and which drives us towards an unrealistic notion of perfection. When we do not achieve as much as others or when we do not meet our own expectation of ourselves, we fall into the trap of judgment in exactly the same way we do when other people fail to meet our expectations. We must learn to be gentle with ourselves and with others. It does not matter what we achieve in material terms; the most important aspect of our growth is how we relate to ourselves and to others.

This is why relationships are such a powerful reflection of what is going on within us. The demands we put on others are a reflection of the demands we put on ourselves – often unrealistic, harking back to the primeval guilt and fear of separation within our race which continuously pushes us forward to prove ourselves. We are often hardest on those closest to us, for they are often mirrors to us. Be aware of how much you judge them, in particular your parents and family, as you will probably be judging a part of yourself.

For some people, this is a very difficult time in relationships. Change occurs at some point in any relationship. When two people change together, it can be a wonderful growing and shared experience; however, change can sometimes be a very painful experience when it occurs in one person and not in the other. However much you try, you cannot expect your partner, family member or friend to see things the way you see them; indeed, in trying to do so, you are trying to control them, for each individual has their own path to follow, which is completely subjective. If you are expecting someone close to you to see something 'your way', then you are behaving in exactly the same way as a totalitarian ruler who imposes rigid laws upon his subjects.

In this time of individual growth, the way we deal with our close relationships is the ultimate test of whether we choose to adhere to the old ways of control and power or follow the path of Love. In the former, we expect our close and dear ones to behave according to what we think is right rather than according to what is right for them. In the latter, we understand that, even if we think we know what is better for the other person, this is irrelevant. We can advise; we can express love; but we cannot interfere with that essential part of the human condition which ensures that each individual has the free will to make their own choices.

In this mass of humanity, we all have our individual decisions to make. The collective decision of mankind, with few dissenting voices, has been, until now, to pursue the straight and narrow path of material progress, which has created the illusion that the material world is the only reality. For those of you who know within yourselves that the only important reality is the world of your own conscience and feelings, your relationship with yourself, your fellow beings and some greater reality which your rational mind cannot comprehend – then, for you, this is where it is natural for your energy to go.

However, the majority of the people you see around you still remain embedded in the material world and this is where they will continue to put their energy until the coming economic collapse will sweep away this blanket of physical security upon which they have always depended. For them, such a collapse will be a traumatic event, but will be the impetus that they require to find that deeper inner core which has remained hidden so long. This is why it is important for all of us to get used to surrounding ourselves with only the bare essentials we need to survive.

It is still time for us to remain centred within our personal world, working on ourselves and learning the true power of Love. It is a Universal Law that every action has an equal reaction and the time is coming when the effect of everything we put out in thought, word and deed will return to us instantly. Such is the energy sweeping through our lives at this moment.

If at any time the path seems lonely, understand not only that there are many others going along the same path in every continent, but also that there are many beings not on this earthly plane who are working with us. Whether you see them as spiritual guides, departed ones or sources of energy does not matter; we are not alone and we are being guided along our path by those who see the whole picture clearer than we do. Learn patience! Eventually, there will come a time when we can step forward with thousands of others to start laying the foundation stones for a new harmonious order based on Love, but we will only be able to do this if we have been working on building this same foundation within our own lives.

Spiritual Living on the Physical Plane II

Denise Cooney

So, physically, what can you do? First take stock and inventory of your body. Short of physical handicaps that truly may cause you not to be able to exercise every muscle in your body, look carefully at every nook and cranny of your body. Do you love it or do you hate it?

If you hate your body, stop right there! Who created that body in the first place? If it is self imposed overweight, that hatred is transfered right to yourself and will affect the performance of the body in its capability to fend off disease and go back into shape. I am not talking about a worldly view of shape or beauty; I am talking about a sacredness that you have forgotten. You are an integral part of the Universe. There is no one like you in this world. You were created by Spirit with a specific purpose and a job and lesson to fulfil and, if you cannot get past the physical, then you will not be able to be clear enough to work on yourself and hear the light and dark that reside within your being.

First step: take a warm bath or shower. Prepare it the way it was done in antiquity. With purpose and ceremony. Clean your bathroom, bring in fragrances and candles. Play some soft music. Close the curtains, turn off the telephone and enter the bath or shower and feel the water cleansing your body. Close your eyes and feel the warmth of the water surrounding your body.

Water is sacred. It represents the subconscious mind and

it also represents the most powerful substance on the earth besides Love.

Allow yourself to drift and place your thoughts into seeing yourself for who you are. Look at yourself; are your intentions during the day for the highest and best of all concerned? Do you surround yourself with Love that is so overwhelming that nothing can move you? Do you have bitterness and resentment over situations? Are you filled with fear, sorrow or lack of faith?

Just allow yourself to drift into whatever energy is all pervasive around your spirit and mind. Focus in on the situation that has been the most resistant in your mind. Allow the situation to play out to the very end. Search deep into yourself for what you are the most of. If it is fear, then go deep into the fear and let it play itself out. Once you discover what it is that has been keeping you frozen in fear, open your eyes and give thanks to the fear for revealing itself to you. Then, bless the very focus of the fear. The reason for this is that all of our emotions seem to have a life of their own. We empower them as if they are living people. Just look at how much stimulation you feel from situations in your life as you retell them to someone else! You get pushed right back into the scene and are feeling the same anger, resentment, fear, pain etc. as before. These are the very things that keep you away from your strength. These are the very things that block the power within yourself from revealing itself to you and sustaining you.

So, if the only person reliving this is you, why allow that situation to keep you prisoner over and over again? You are not getting even or even if you elicit a feeling of sympathy from the person you are sharing this emotion with, has it indeed changed the situation or circumstances? Absolutely not! This is what is known as the dark side. It is the power we all have as well as the Light within ourselves.

So, once you have engaged in the water ceremony and have seen the blessing and the releasing from within, the next step is not only to bless the situation but also to embrace the fear, anger, pain etc. and let it go. Tell it you recognize its sacredness in your life. (For after all, haven't you given it god-like status by letting it run your life?) You also let it know that you need it to be in your life for the useful purpose it was actually put here for. Let the fear warn you of impending danger, rather than disabling you and paralyzing you against experiencing courage. Let anger know that you likewise need its power to move you to become active in life to create change. For example, if you are furious over the Earth and her condition, just call on the healthy side of anger to motivate you to **do something about it** instead of just sitting there complaining and being angry over life in general. You can call on the dark side of yourself to assist you to move. But be aware! The dark side is very powerful and do not think you can wish or trick it away.

You must recognize that we are both sides and we must focus in on integrating ourselves and not feel scared by any one aspect of ourselves.

After you bless yourself, then go into the world and become more focused in on who you are. Act like an outside observer of yourself. Make no judgement of yourself and just be a witness to all that you do. Then, focus in at night and take mental inventory of how you handled situations and allow yourself to see that you must bless this as well. You must stop judging what you do as failure or fool yourself into being trapped by the ego and saying: 'Gee! I have this situation licked'. The Universe has a sneaky way of testing you. Just when you get all filled up with ego gas, you get popped.

So, start seeing everything you do as sacred. This will change the way you handle your life. When you arise, give thanks for the day. Don't look at your alarm clock and say: 'Only a few more minutes'. Bless your body before you even get out of bed. Bless your life. Whether you have a partner or not, bless the people in your life especially the ones that you feel are inferior to you in any way. Bless your food. Realize that you have something to eat and see all that was involved in bringing it to you. Bless all the people responsible for providing you with your food. And so on and so on.

When you understand that life is not out to get you but rather you are to get into life, all types of doorways open up. Stop feeling sorry for yourself! If there are things you cannot resolve through meditation or prayer, go and seek counselling from a therapist. There are many sincere seekers of Truth who offer their services. Of course, look for someone who is in alignment with your belief system. They are out there. Just because you learn to release and let go on the spiritual level, you may still have an intense residue that needs to be scrubbed by a different type of cleanser on the emotional level. So never be ashamed to seek help whether it is medical or psychological.

Another way to release which is very important to work with is taking a blank piece of paper and a black pen and writing to the Angel of your Higher Self and then writing with full force all of the things that have bothered you. By writing, you are releasing things from the internal mind and putting them into physical form so that they can be released into the spiritual realm. This is a very powerful form of healing. I recommend that you have a copper pot or a metal pot that you use for this purpose alone. I have worked with this and have found it very effective. When you do this meditation, make sure you re-read the entire sheet or sheets of paper to include all of the hurt and anger that resides within you. If something comes up after you read it over, rewrite it onto the sheets. After you are satisfied that all of your violent hatred or anger or resentment or pain has been the Master of your life for all these years, then write on the bottom that you release this to free yourself and all that you have imprisoned. Crumple each piece of paper very sincerely and silently. Think of the release. Then, using stick matches, burn this. You must watch the flames burn, as you will see the most incredible things. Then try to think of it no more. If you must, do this daily until you feel the situations leaving your life one by one.

This is something that I had learned from a woman who is a very powerful teacher of Truth, only later to discover that Mexican Indians, of which I am descended, use this in their ceremony as well.

These are only a few of the many wonderful releasing processes that you can do for yourself. The only other one which I feel is safe and with which you cannot harm yourself is to go to the Water. Whether it is a stream or whether it is a river or ocean, the spirit of the Water is the same. The Water is a very powerful spirit and force – you do not play with any spirits for entertainment or just because you read about them, I must emphasize this. Do not underestimate the damage you can do to yourself in fooling around with power. The Water is to be respected. Address the Water. Let the Water know you have some problems which need to be resolved. Then, silently or verbally, throw into the Water all of the thoughts that you need to release. After you spend time releasing, feel the healing energy of the Water as it washes over your soul. Thank the Water for your healing, then proceed to clean up the area around you of any debris.

With all of the changes that are happening on the Earth, it is so important that you clean up your act and get ready to do your work. Whatever that is. All work is spiritual and you must allow yourself to see that your job is very important. It provides you with a source of income. You must be willing to tithe that income to a source that gives you great spiritual understanding and upliftment. Give approximately 10% of your income to a spiritual group or person or whatever. You will see increase. Tithe 10% of your time to making the world a better place to live. Work or volunteer with Earthday committees, children, shelters, etc. Give back to the Planet. Also, prepare yourself for the changes by giving up your credit and start paying off your debt. I cannot emphasize the importance of this. You must pay off your debt.

Look for other people of like mind. Be aware of the New Agers who say all of this is negative thinking. If you go and see a doctor because you don't feel well and he or she turns you away because you have really negative symptoms, how are you to be healed? There is the Old Way of doing things.

This is known as the Sacred Path. It takes dedicated and hardworking people to do this type of work. You must be ready to do work at the cost of leaving all you know behind. What price are you willing to pay for your freedom from the endless cycles of karma? If all of this was painless and easy, I doubt if humanity as a whole would engage in this pursuit of spiritual awareness and change over the Earth. It is not without some human sacrifice. Once you see what you have gained, it is worth the freedom. Just think of it as knowing what is going to happen all around you and being guided so that none of the harm comes to you, always being at the right place at the right time.

Of all the blessings I can count on, it is that I am Divinely Protected in every single phase of my life. I have been in very humanly dangerous situations and have been safe. I have been in very dangerous weather conditions and have been protected. There is not one situation where I feel that the God/Goddess Spirit has not taken full charge over my life and given me opportunity to despair; but I have chosen to see the Higher Path and have been relieved of all sorrow.

Let me give a personal example. Recently I gave birth to a beautiful son. All throughout the pregnancy, I told him of the dangers on our Earth and warned him that this was a very precarious time to be born and, if he chose to leave this world, I would understand. I was with the most wonderful midwives. The labor was hard but not unbearable. Understanding meditation and breathing assisted me in going through 13 hours of labor. I visualized what was happening throughout the process. I had spent months reading and rereading the exact physiological process so that I would be mentally prepared for the physical changes. This helped tremendously. Yet, at the final moments when I was bearing down, we lost his heartbeat. We were at a Birthing Center and needed to go to the hospital post haste. So they called for an ambulance and we were off to the hospital. They told me to stop pushing. The midwife, Lonny, kept telling me everything would be fine. Yet she had a tone of anxiety in her voice, so I knew it might not be O.K.

This is where I felt the peace of Spirit overtake me. All the way to the hospital, I kept saying to myself 'Thy Will Be Done. In Me, Through Me and For Me.'

I was totally resigned in courage and strength that the Divine Will of Spirit knew greater than I. If it meant the sacrifice of my baby, then so be it. This was not from a place of sorrow, lamenting, victimized martyrdom, or giving up. This is true surrender. Needless to say, I gave birth to a baby who was very much alive. This is the type of surrender and strength we need to exhibit in our lives.

So many times when you hear the word surrender, people feel they must be the victim who is being held up by the big, bad bandit. They react in the same way when you use the words of forgiveness and letting go. 'What is the reason for standing and taking it?' Please understand that even when you are releasing and letting go, it does not guarantee that you have yet been entirely freed from your situation.

You need to understand that there are certain family situations which are for the highest and best of all. What needs to change is your attitude towards them. If there is control or domination by parents, in-laws, spouses or family in general, then you need to become strong and let yourself be plugged in no more. Learn to take the stance of someone who is no longer willing to attend functions just because it is expected of you. Learn that family is a blood tie that can be released. It is far more important for one to be in a healthy environment with people whom we love than to be with *family* because it is expected of us. Our Spiritual Family are our friends with whom we associate and share love for the Earth and respect for themselves.

So what does this have to do with you or the Earth changes? Many things. There will be situations in your life that you cannot change. So you must learn to empower yourself. Learn to hear the inner voice and be guided by it. You can hear that inner voice if you choose to listen carefully. It will open up doors of wisdom that you never knew existed within. There will be many more things happening around you. You too may have to leave family behind.

Our dream state is very powerful. Within our dreams are usually the normal daily dreams of working out the past day and then there are dreams of Prophecy. How you work with yourself on a daily level will allow these dreams to speak to you. Start keeping a diary by your bed and, after you have blessed yourself, write down or tell your dream to someone so that you remember it. You can learn a lot of important things in the dream state. I ask the Angels of Sleep to reveal the Truth of situations to me when I have a situation that does not resolve itself with my logical mind. Sometimes, I try to take so much control over working out a situation that I forget to ask for help from the available resources around me and the only way that I can hear an answer is in the sleep state when my logical(?) mind is shut off. Then, Spirit sends me the answers in the most wonderful way. I also face up to the scary parts of my dream by letting it know that this is only a dream and to go away. It takes a lot of practice to be in charge, knowing that you are asleep. This has taken me years to do but if you don't start sometime, you will never master this within yourself.

When you finally see that you are your own salvation, that you are your own Teacher Within and that all knowledge resides within you, you can then start learning from the school of life and start seeing that life is not filled with misery but with lessons, so that we might improve ourselves and attain our birthright which is Godhood.

Be honest with yourself about who you are and your limitations. There cannot be enough emphasis on this. I have read about visualization and some people think it is the cure all. For some things, it seems to create a healing. Please do not dupe yourself into thinking that you can visualize yourself into something that you are not. You can visualize to create a shift, but all the visualization in the world will not bring you wealth. You still need to take the responsibility to make things happen for yourself. It is a tool, not a lucky rabbit's foot to make things materialize out of nothing. Yes. It can work to heal disease by working the mind; but it is your own physical body that you are healing and if you continue to stay ill, this does not mean that you have failed.

Visualizations are the most abused and misinformed powers that the New Age set has delivered to the public. When you think about it, you have been given a very powerful tool to change things. This borders on manipulation of the world and the environment around you. Given the wrong set of information on this power, you could actually with a good heart try to change someone else's life. If you are successful in bringing change to someone or something, that is none of your business anyway – then you have abused the power and incurred new karma for yourself to work out. Be careful with visualizations; keep them for healing yourself and be careful about what you are asking for. Do you have the right to ask for it and can you handle the responsibility that comes with forcefully changing your destiny?

These are just things to think about. My Guides have been very clear that this is the time to work on yourself and to find yourself a really good teacher – someone who will assist you to work on yourself, but one who, if they teach you occult skills, they teach you to respect those skills and the repercussions of abuse of power. Even if you think you are helping someone else, isn't it up to you to ask for their highest and best good and not to direct or orchestrate for them what you believe their highest and best should be?

Everyone falls into this trap at some point in their spiritual growth unless they have a teacher with them to bop them over the head, to warn them of the folly of their ways.

Finding yourself a teacher would be a very good idea. Be open and ask them how they have come to their conclusions. No teacher should appear to be unapproachable. They need also to live what they teach to the best of their capability.

The following information that I will give you is some of the channeled information that my guides have revealed to a few of the groups that I work with. I trust that you have found this information helpful to you.

I ask that you are opened to the Truth and may Spirit guide you to the Highest and Best on your Path. If you are practicing Truth already, I trust this will be of further assistance on your Path. May you enjoy the blessings of every experience in your life and learn to unravel the mysteries so they become demystified for you to live your life to the best of your capability.

The World of Illusion

Denise Cooney

We are going to start with a prayer of affirmation. We also ask that the energy of the moon and the goddess nature of the moon as well as the god nature of the sun and the nature of the Divine Beingness and the Divine Christ consciousness make its way into your hearts to create a balance and a healing.

No matter how many times we say it, you have to really understand that there is going to be a great exodus of physical life from this planet into the ethers. It doesn't really sound like it's actually sunk in to the main gist of humanity. Nor does it sound as if it's actually focused in or sunk in to people, individuals working on their own spirituality. The more you really understand that, the more you will understand that you may not know that day you are going to make the transition, but your transition could be very imminent, not from a negative standpoint, but rather because the earth is going through that cleansing.

Between the things that are happening on the physical plane, albeit through your pollution, through your lack of care, through your disease process, this is the way that the earth is going to clean itself. And, the thing that you have to really take a look at is what is really important for you, your individual growth and your spiritual growth. This is why we keep repeating in different ways, shapes and forms, not to worry about your family, not to worry about your friends.

Take the energy source you have left here on the earth and focus in on your own spiritual development, focus in on looking at the parts of yourself that are finite, the parts of yourself that are working to reach towards that infinite part of yourself. Look and dwell on your spirituality and try, as best you can, not to get caught up in the physical plane.

The physical plane, whether it's a home, whether it's a family, whether it's relationships, that is not what's going to carry you through the transition. They, for the most part, can literally be the obstacles that keep you away from really focusing in on Higher Source and really allowing yourself to bring Higher Truth through.

Now, we are not saying that you are going to become a recluse; nor are we saying that you become so individualized that you do not enjoy the physical plane, but what we're saying is that now is not the time to obsess; now is the time for balance. And you are going to find different parts of your personality, different aspects, for each and every one of you are going to be a hook, a certain type of hook, which consistently and constantly is going to pull you away from the main gist of your journey, because it's your personality self, the one that you claim with your name. It's your personality self that tells you: 'Well! I know all these things are happening, but I am important, I am extremely important, I am more important than what is happening, because I have too much to do'.

Let's say you go to see the doctor and it's a guarantee you only have two years to live. You have two years to live, this is all the time you have left, and you know it's not going to be through slow deterioration. The doctor said: 'Well, look, you're going to die. There is a lot in two years, your life force is over, that's it!' Are you going to spend the next two years of your life, then, obsessing over situations in your life, really trying to push your point upon somebody else, or are you going to be so focused in on the things that are around you and reattune your hearing, reattune your feelings, reattune your eyes, reattune your entire emotional beingness into the joy of the sunrise and the sunset, to the joy in the mysticism of seeing the moon, to the absolute exhilaration that you have all these different types of techniques within yourself to call upon higher spirit, different spirits that exist, and to really commune with nature?

The drug of this world of illusion is so strong, it makes you forget that you only come here to grow spiritually. It makes you forget so well, that your whole focus becomes, in the modern day, your television, your newspaper, little heroes and little heroines who put themselves up on a pedestal, or villains who want to turn people into victims. You sit there and you love to hate and criticize because of what they are trying to do to mislead people, yet you as an individual do absolutely nothing to try to undo that; you just pour more hatred into the situation. It is a really amazing drug, the world of illusion; it makes you forget that beyond the illusion is reality, so that you even think your relationships are real, you even think your physical life is real.

You really need to rework and relearn once again; this is why you started your meditation or whatever techniques you know. The techniques are minor; the techniques are like a diamond tool trying to cut through something so that you can get to the gem which is on the inside. You can apply the tool over and over again, but, if you see the gem and you don't know its worth, then the tool is of no use. Use the tools you have to understand yourself psychologically. Use the tools you have to understand yourself emotionally. Use the tools you have to understand yourself spiritually, but more importantly, use the main tool, and understand and remind yourself, like in *The Wizard of Oz*, that you're sleeping, that this world of illusion is a dream. The more you remember, the more you will awaken yourself.

If you choose to have families or relationships, do it if that's what you're doing, but don't get so caught up and think this is it, this is all of it, my job, my age, my relationships, this is all I have to live for. If that's all you have to live for, you are really still making small steps on the spiritual path, but better to make small steps on the spiritual path and consciously work on the spiritual path than none at all. See! Everyone is on the spiritual path. Everyone is created by God, everything that you see is from Divine Beingness. When you as an individual go into judgement and become judge, jury and executioner of people and situations around yourself, this is how you will be judged when you go into transition and you look how harshly you have judged things around you. To become impartial will help free you up so much from the bonds of karma, from the endless wheel of birth and death.

The world of illusion and the ego are an incredibly strong bond. This is what makes you want to seek partnership, this is what makes you want to seek power, this is what makes you want to seek occupation. This is what makes you seek these things, even if you say I am not seeking this, on some level you are seeking it. This is how subtle the ego can be. When you say, 'I am good', this is the ego speaking. When you say 'I am bad', this is the ego speaking. When 'I have superior intelligence', this is the ego speaking. When 'I have inferior intelligence or inferior ways of doing things', this is the ego speaking. Ego enjoys being separate from the whole. There is such a source of enjoyment of being separate when in reality there is no separation between you and the whole, and at the same time there is this frustration: 'How do I get back to the Divine Oneness that I want to attain?' In order to be a vessel, you have to look at world events, no matter what is happening, and say: 'This, too, shall pass. This is the world of illusion. This is here to awaken humanity, to allow humanity to see that this absolutely has no meaning whatsoever.'

What can you do? You make a stand, you make a stand in your own home, you make a stand in your own life, you make a stand within your own consciousness. If you can't do anything, you make a stand to focus in on seeing that this is an illusion, this is a transitory situation, and if you see that there is nothing you can do, say to yourself, truthfully: 'There is nothing I can do; I cannot stay attached to the situation. I need to move forward. What can I work on?' And it's not that you become an individual who just becomes passive and lets everything happen to you; you do work with action. But, within the action, within the framework that you can work within, now is not the time to hate people, now is not the time to hold grudges, now is not the time to want to get even and, if that is what you want to do more than anything else, to prove your point, to show you're right, then you are allowing yourself crucial moments in the Divine newness of it all. You are showing yourself to yourself, to your higher self, what is really more important. It is not the search for God, it is the completion of what the ego has set itself out to do, which is to prove something. And what are you proving within the world of illusion? The world of illusion, as much as you prove, will give you other things to prove. It is like a drug addict. It is a drug. The more you do the drug, the more you need the drug, the more you need to do. Unlike a person who overdoses and dies, you don't die from this drug. You stay immersed in it, but the type that you have is the death that prevents you from really living life to its fullest: which is being in the oneness and going beyond this plane of consciousness so that at that point you do work with the Higher Teachers, with the Higher Masters working to assist others.

It is very hard and it's a very lonely path. The higher you go, the fewer the numbers, the more barren the path. The steeper it gets, the more you feel you are going to fall off, but you won't. But, it feels very lonely. And that's another thing, because the ego doesn't like to be alone, the ego doesn't want to know ahead of time that you are going to feel lonely; it's a temporary loneliness. It's purely temporary, momentary. It happens just for a blink of an eye. And, it's not a punishment, it's just the higher you go in altitude, the harder it is to breath the air. What you're doing, the higher you go in your spiritual altitude, the fresher the consciousness, the fewer the people who have made the journey, the more open the atmosphere, the more dizzying the heights, because now you are entering into an area that says you are really taking responsibility for who you are and very few people venture that far.

You're just going through the motions of completion. Everything you start out to do has already been completed. You're just making the motions towards the completion. But, you understand, as soon as you have a thought, that thought becomes a desire, the desire becomes a reality and it's already finished. What you put into motion has already ended; you're just allowing yourself to walk towards it. Because, no matter what you do, you had a thought of birth and the completion of your birth is your death; you're only walking towards your death every second. So, whatever you start, if it's a job, you're only walking towards the end of the job at some point. You start a relationship, one of you is either going to die or somebody is going to leave. You've already completed what you started. You know you bought a car, some day you're going to pay it off, some day it'll be yours. Whatever you start, it's already completed. If you start working towards your God-goodness realization, towards understanding higher truth, it has already been completed. Just keep your focus, so that you have that completion totally in your hands.

The only moment you're ever alive is right now and that's the only moment you're going to be alive in the future. You're just walking towards the completion of the beginning of the end; this is why this is the finite world. In reality, nothing begins, nothing ends, everything just is. So, you think too small; we are trying to have you think a little bit larger so that you can see this.

What you really need to understand is that the only thing that exists in the Universe is **Truth** and **Love**. And it just is. If you can really understand that. In this physical plane you have hatred, you have animosity, you have anger, you have jealousy, you have the distorted images of truth. You have some real glimmering of truth, some kind of feeling of love, but it's only when you connect with God that you really do feel love. Human being love to human being love is not superior Love. It is a type of love, but it is not love in the pure sense. It is also intertwined with lust and it is also intertwined with conditions. But, there is always an ulterior something somewhere, you can't help it. That's par for your human nature. But, to love one other person unconditionally is so rare, we can say there have been four who have done so since the beginning of your human history. So, if you fool yourself: 'Oh, no! I love unconditionally', but then let your partner do something you don't like and then you get upset, that's not unconditional love. But, 'I forgave them immediately!'; it's still not unconditional love. It was unconditional until they did something that broke your unconditional condition. You don't even love yourself unconditionally. You have all these rules and regulations about how far you'll go and what you'll do and what you're all about!

So, the thing is that you're here to live, you're here to enjoy, you're here to experience and you're here to really remember that this is nothing at all. It's to really see that it's a dream and, when you can see this, you're free.

Bibliography

The literature touching in one way or another on all the matters of human evolution, the ancient past and the future prospects of our planet, is so voluminous that we can mention only some of the most important works that we have consulted. Many of them are no longer in print but are available from public libraries. The BIBLE, the QURAN (KORAN) and many other well-known Holy Books of various religions have also been much researched in addition to the list which now follows.

BABA, Meher
Discourses

BAMFORTH, Nick
AIDS & The Healer Within
Duality Into Unity (1992 publication)
Trusting The Healer Within

CAMPBELL, Joseph
Occidental Mythology
Oriental Mythology
Primitive Mythology
plus many other works

COONEY, Denise
Beyond A Master

COUNTRYMAN, J.
Atlantis & The Seven Stars

DANIKEN, Erich von
Chariots of the gods
and numerous follow-up books.

DUNNE, J. W.
An Experiment with Time
The New Immortality
Nothing Dies
The Serial Universe
Intrusions?

FITZWALTER, Bernard, & HENRY, Raymond
Dark Stars

GOOCH, Stan
The Double Helix of the Mind
Guardians of the Ancient Wisdom
The Neanderthal Question
Personality and Evolution
Total Man.

HAICH, Elizabeth
Initiations

HOYLE, Fred
The Intelligent Universe

JUNG, C. G.
Flying Saucers.

MORSE, Eric
The Living Stars

MUCK, Otto
The Secret of Atlantis

SANTILLANA & VON DECHEND
  Hamlet's Mill

STREIBER, Whitley
  Communion – A True Story

THEDRA, Sister
  Intercom: Messages from the Realm of Light

WELLS, H. G.
  Anticipations (publ'd 1902)
  A Short History of the World
  The Time Machine
  The Shape of Things To Come
  plus many other works, fiction and non-fiction.

Trusting
the
Healer Within

NICK BAMFORTH

Dis-ease is evident everywhere in our society, whether manifesting itself as physical sickness, emotional pain or psychological imbalance. Yet, in our personal lives, it is when we are physically and emotionally at our lowest ebb that we are forced to look deep within ourselves and thereby have the greatest potential to create change and growth in our lives.

TRUSTING THE HEALER WITHIN was written to guide the reader towards this inner transformation. Whether we are confronted by a serious illness such as cancer or Aids or whether we are going through a period of emotional turmoil, stagnation or alienation, we all have the power to heal ourselves in the deepest sense.

TRUSTING THE HEALER WITHIN is in two parts.
Understanding The Healer Within explains the emotional and physical forces which bring imbalance into our lives and focuses on the nature of dis-ease as a means of stimulating us towards a greater awareness of our inner potential.
Practicing The Healer Within focuses on the most common causes of dis-ease and, with the help of specific meditations, guides the reader towards a renewed state of inner harmony and faith in The Healer Within: the ability to create one's own reality, health and well-being.

Beyond
A
Master

DENISE COONEY

So much has been said and written about the coming of the so-called 'New Age', but how does this really relate to our own lives? What are the changes that will occur and are indeed occurring at this very moment in time?

What we are going through at this moment is the return of the Christ Consciousness to this planet, a gradual shifting from the power vibration which has been the hallmark of this planet for the past two thousand years to the heart vibration of love, which is our true birthright.

This book consists of channelled information by Sananda, the new name of the Christ vibration entering the physical level of the Earth, and by Sanat Kumara, the unifying force of our Solar System. On a spiritual, yet also practical level they explain how we as individuals must prepare for and, indeed become part of the coming changes. It focuses in particular on how we have the power within us to create not only our own reality but also the future of this planet – how to guide the Earth from its present vibration of power into her rightful energy of the heart.

SANAT KUMARA speaks: 'Humanity must understand the reason why everyone at this moment in time has such a feeling of anticipation. That anticipation is a letting go of old thoughts, a letting go of the old way, and allowing the person's personality self and ego to be released so that each and every individual on the planet Earth opens himself up to become a Divine Instrument.

The
Living
Stars

DR ERIC MORSE

All of us have at some time looked with an overwhelming sense of awe at the stars on a clear night, wondering what really lies behind those twinkling lights.

This book explores more deeply than ever before the time-honoured notions of how we humans relate, or should relate, to the greater life force that stars imply to us. Based within a framework of the most up-to-date astronomical knowledge, the approach taken here is necessarily astrological, deciphering the meaning of man's living relationship to the stars and the Universe as a whole.

The principal emphasis of the book is:
- Man's relationship to the stars and, in particular, the need to understand what particular impulses we derive from them. The traditional view is that most stars have a malefic effect on humanity; this book destroys this myth and shows how *all* stars can be applied to benefic purposes.
- Which stars are important (out of millions) and why. The traditional choice is largely haphazard.
- The many folklores of stars – different cultures and different ages. Which of these are relevant now?
- The physics of stars as creative forces in the universe and in ourselves.
- An ephermis of the main stars (about 130).